Heidi Heaven Bound

A Families Journey Through Grief

MARSHA R. NIX

TATE PUBLISHING, LLC

"Heidi Heaven Bound" by Marsha R. Nix
Copyright © 2005 by Marsha R. Nix. All rights reserved.

Published in the United States of America
by Tate Publishing, LLC
127 East Trade Center Terrace
Mustang, OK 73064
(888) 361–9473

Book design copyright © 2005 by Tate Publishing, LLC. All rights reserved.

No part of this publication may be reproduced, stored in a retrieval system or transmitted in any way by any means, electronic, mechanical, photocopy, recording or otherwise without the prior permission of the author except as provided by USA copyright law.

Scripture quotations marked "NIV" are taken from the *Holy Bible, New International Version* ®, Copyright © 1973, 1978, 1984 by International Bible Society. Used by permission of Zondervan Publishing House. All rights reserved.

This book is designed to provide accurate and authoritative information with regard to the subject matter covered. This information is given with the understanding that neither the author nor Tate Publishing, LLC is engaged in rendering legal, professional advice. Since the details of your situation are fact dependent, you should additionally seek the services of a competent professional.

ISBN: 1–5988616–7-0

Dedication

This book is dedicated to my children, Michelle and Larry who are truly blessings in my life and to my grandchildren, Dylan, Hayley, Haydon, Colin and Torey of whom are my Grand blessings and to my granddaughter in heaven Heidi with whom one day I will again share a *home*.

Acknowledgement

While writing this book it became abundantly clear to me the importance of the people God has placed in my life, each one for a special purpose, each one to fulfill His purpose. This book would have never been written without their encouragement, love, and support through all of the difficult days, through all the tears.

God's support team has been our Life Group from Eastside Christian Church in Fullerton, California. They have truly been a rock in my life. This group of loving people has shown me what it means to be fearless, bold, and faithful. Their hugs, words of encouragement and prayers for healing, mercy and reconciliation have given me strength to continue. With outstretched hands of love, no matter how or where my life has gone, this wonderful God-sent Life Group has given me the freedom to share and be authentic with them and this has made my burden lighter.

This is not just a group of people, they are truly my "family" and I treasure them beyond words.

> *"Two are better than one, because they have a good return for their work: If one falls down his friend can help him up. But pity the man who falls and has no one to help him up! Also, if two lie down together, they will keep warm. But how can one keep warm alone? Though one may be overpowered, two can defend themselves. A cord of three strands is not quickly broken." Ecclesiastes 4:9–12 (NIV)*

A book cannot be completed without someone taking the time to read and re-read it over and over again. My daughter Michelle has spent many hours helping me put my thoughts together and then making sure those thoughts were understandable. Without her support and love this book would have never made it to final submission. She put time aside from a busy schedule of raising four children, as a single mother to leaf through pages of paper and submission guidelines and for this I am not only thankful but also richly blessed. She is the true writer in the family and I hope one day to be able to help with her book.

There are so many others who have encouraged me, prayed with and for me, and enabled me to keep my focus on God. I thank each person, of whom it would take pages to mention by name, that has taken time from busy schedules to let me cry, let me vent, whether it be on the phone, over lunch or at dinner and sometimes just hold me. There are many who have kept my family lifted up in prayer and reached beyond friendship not only to hold me up spiritually but also to hold me up physically. Without these true God-sent blessings, these angels of mercy, I would not have been able to remain standing. I will be eternally grateful and forever friends.

This book was written on business trips, vacations, in the office, and at home while tears ran down my face like water crashing down a waterfall. Sometimes there was more Kleenex around me than paper. My husband of forty years, Larry Sr., let me have time and space to work through my thoughts, hurts and fears. Through much of this process our marriage has been put on hold and I cannot express my feelings of love and gratitude to him for giving me this "space". Without his support this book would have never come to fruition. He was the first to read it and the first to encourage me to share it. He is my biggest cheerleader. He is truly my best friend and love of my life.

Table of Contents

Foreword 9
Preface 11
Who is in Charge? 15
Seeing With God's Eyes 25
Focus on the Gift 35
Everyone in Their Place 43
Clothed in Glory, Covered in Fear 55
Running, Falling, Just Keep Moving 67
The Train of Survival 77
Heidi and Her Hugs 83
One Big Happy Family 91
Where Do We Go From Here 95
Split in Half 101
The Truth and Nothing but the Truth
   So Help Me God 109
Haydon, the Survivor 115
Trusting the System or Trusting God 119
Shattered Lives 123
A Life Time in One Year 131
Building Up and Falling Apart 135
Teach me to do Your Will 143
Your Journey 149
Heidi Heaven Bound 151
Epilogue 155

Foreword

When the phone rings and on the other end devastation, hurt, and painful loss that is beyond description awaits you–*you have a choice*–"do I run from God or do I run to Him?" To run to Him means not only to run to His promises but also to embrace His truth **and** live it each day. It is no easy path (that is for sure), but it is the way that leads to healing and hope, and most of all *His wonderful hug!*

In the pages that follow, Marsha Nix bares her soul as she walks in the valley and shares her families journey into grief, heartache, and wrestling with that decision each one must make about *running to* or *from God.* Without a doubt the stormy and difficult pilgrimage with the Lord that you are about to read will help *you* in *your* life story or with *your* phone call of anguish and grief. I know . . . I was there that fateful morning and in the days that followed. I've seen what God can do when you choose to let Him . . . and also when you don't.

Marsha, who is just like you or me, is no super-Christian, famous author or conference speaker. She is a wife, a mother, a grandmother and a businesswoman who loves the Lord as she struggles through one of life's most devastating tragedies. Her desire to grow in the Lord is very strong as she seeks the best for herself, her family, her friends, for you the reader and most importantly, *for Jesus Christ!*

Some things in life make sense and other things

may never make sense in this very broken world. Still one thing is clear–to hold on to God's Hand each and every moment of life's journey *makes all the difference in this world and the next!* Just ask Marsha . . .

God bless you when you embrace that life-filling truth as you turn each heartfelt page and discover what *REAL* trust, love, and loss is all about.

Dave Higgins, Pastor
Eastside Christian Church
Romans 8:28–29

Preface

> *"And we know that in all things God works for the good of those who love him, who have been called according to his purpose."* Romans 8:28 (NIV)

This is a story of my journey through the valley of grief; the depth of loss and the road back to life, to hope. It is the true story of my family; your average dysfunctional family shattered like Humpty Dumpty when tragedy strikes. It is the story of how God is putting the pieces back together again one painful graft at a time.

It all started with the death of my eight-year-old granddaughter Heidi. It is told from my point of view and how I felt, how I feel, my thoughts on God, and how I have grieved and how I continue, with God's help, to go on. It is my recollection of a few of the events that tore my family apart and how each member of the family is continuing on their own journey. There were many other crises that happened during this time, many things that happened were truly unbelievable to those who watched us and helped us. Events that affected all of us, but I have selected the stories that stand out as the most deeply felt and influential at that time.

This story is not meant to place blame or judgment on any one person for judgment is in God's hands and, forgiveness is in mine. It is not meant to open up wounds that just now have scabbed over and are continuing to heal but to offer a view from the valleys of life, the process of healing, reconciliation, and forgiveness. Every person who has lost a child goes through a deep grieving process. All are difficult, all are different, but not all tear a family apart. Loosing a child goes beyond life changing, it is heart-changing and soul changing.

If you were to ask each person in this story how the events went for them they would each shed a different light on the same event. I would hope this story would encourage each of them to write their thoughts down and share them; it has been a huge part of my healing process. There are losses in life that you never "get over," you learn to continue on. You learn that continuing is a choice, a choice that honors the child you lost. This is my view from my walk, my journey that God has taken me on through the valley. I have learned that only by walking in the valleys of life can you deeply appreciate the mountaintop experiences.

We all talk about our problems, losses, and life challenges and we all say, "We'll get through it." I believe we are to do more than that; we are to get "above" it. When you go through something you come out on the other side and can view it only as the world sees it. It is important to get through our valleys and it is equally important to then move above it. Our trials are meant to grow our faith in a deeper way, a higher way then we ever knew. We are meant to get above the valley, above the depths of darkness, and see with God's eyes. We are meant to see His purpose for our life, in relationship to others.

Our purpose is to love one another even when we are not loveable, to give grace as we receive grace, and not count the times we forgive. We are to praise God for the valleys so our faith can grow. Only then we can reach up, touch the hem of Jesus' robe and understand, as we rise above the hurt, above the pain, that we are loved.

This love is so deep, it reaches around us and up to eternity, love that is unconditional and unfailing by God our Father, our Creator. We are reminded through pain that Jesus Christ died for us and is our Lord and Savoir and just by asking and then letting go He will be our guide here on earth and our guide to take us *home*.

I have been asked many times "what can we do for your family, how can we help you?" My answer is; "pray for us" for in reality that is all anyone can do for another person. It is our job to pray for others, it is the job of the Holy Spirit to change others. I continue to be changed.

> *"I will utter hidden things, things from of old–what we have heard and known, what our fathers have told us. We will not hide them from their children, we will tell the next generation the praiseworthy deeds of the Lord, his power and the wonders he had done. . . . .so the next generation would know them, even the children yet to be born, and they in turn would tell their children. Then they would put their trust in God and would not forget his deeds but would keep his commands. They would not be like their forefathers–a stubborn and rebellious generation, whose hearts were not loyal to God, whose spirits were not faithful to him." Psalm 78: 2–8 (NIV)*

I pray that each person in my family will find their purpose in life and understand how precious the gift of life is, and by doing so not to waste a moment sharing their story and showing God's love. That it does not matter how much money you make, where you live, how much "stuff" you accumulate or what your career choice is, it only matters how much love you give to others. It does not matter how long you live but the contributions you make while you are here on earth. I hope they learn that even though Heidi was young when she died she made a great contribution. She accepted Jesus as her Lord and Savior and opened the hearts of the ones she loved and who loved her to the realization that we are all headed *home*.

Marsha R. Nix
Anaheim, California
2005

Who is in Charge?

Our Plans

The day started out like any other day when traveling for business. It is always a bit on the stressful side when you are away from your own environment. This trip was especially so as it was a quick turn around trip. Getting to the airport and then to your rental car while making sure you have your luggage takes planning and more effort than the normal day at work. This trip to Utah was somewhat unusual and both my son Larry and I felt uncomfortable but neither of us shared our feelings about our apprehension. It ended up being a trip we would never forget, one we would always remember as the most devastating day imaginable. It became a defining moment in our lives and changed not only Larry forever but also our entire family.

Our sales and lead process always began at a trade show and then there was the follow up. The trips and contacts were normally done within the first two months after the show and this was no exception. Larry and I had both contacted CEO's and Presidents of banks located in Utah and Idaho that had stopped by our booth at a trade show in March and we planned to see them on this trip. What was a bit unusual was getting four banks in the area to meet with us all within a two-day time frame. In sales when the iron is hot you go, when there is interest you go, and they were all interested in our products and services. The state of Utah was usually not highly represented at the Western Independent Bankers Presidents Conference. As it was held this particular year in Phoenix, Arizona the banks from Utah had a higher attendance rate. So off to Utah we went with great expectations.

A couple of the bank presidents would not commit to the day and time. They had told us to call when we were in town and they would meet with us. I was not sure that there was a need for me to go. Just seven days prior Larry Sr. and I had returned from taking our two eight-year old granddaughters Heidi, Larry's daughter, and Hayley, Michelle's daughter to Hawaii. We had had a wonderful time and the girls literally had the time of their lives. After a recent trip to Hawaii with our granddaughters and Easter the weekend before, I was not eager to be traveling again.

Larry is very competent and could handle any questions that may be presented by these presidents. I kept thinking there was no need for me to go, yet a small voice inside said, "Go." On Saturday, April 26, 2003 I decided to listen to that voice and to go. As neither of us was feeling secure in this trip, we made our reservations late on Saturday for a one way trip to Salt Lake City, Utah, on a flight out of Orange County Airport on Sunday, April 27th. Uneasiness was flooding both of our minds but it was easily pushed back. We were not sure if we would be back on Tuesday or Wednesday, it would depend on our appointment schedule.

After landing late Sunday we drove to Provo, Utah and spent the night. Larry was the driver and enjoyed the long drives from one place to another, for me the shorter the drive the better. This seemed to me a long drive, as I was tired and still thinking there was no need to be here with Larry on this trip. Our first meeting was in Provo and our next meeting was in a small town outside of Provo. The meetings went well and we were off on another long drive back in the direction of Idaho to spend the night for our next meeting at 9:30 in the morning. On our way we made some phone calls and set up our last meeting at 11:30 on Tuesday. That would put us about 2 hours from Salt Lake City and the airport so we could schedule our return flight. I called Southwest Airlines and scheduled our return flight out of Salt Lake City at 3:30 in the afternoon on Tuesday. That would work great. We arranged for Larry Sr. to pick up Heidi and Haydon from school and drive to the airport to pick us up. They would love to see their Daddy land in an airplane. Heidi loved to run into her Daddy's arms and he loved to catch her and get one of her famous long, soul exchanging hugs. Everything was set, going according to our plans.

God's Plan

Our plans, that is just what they were, but God had His plans for our life and we often forget who is really in charge. So many times when "our plans" get changed or are diverted we have a tendency to blame someone for interfering or even ourselves for not planning better, but usually we look to place blame somewhere else. How many times had I read the story of Moses, Abraham, and David and saw how God's plan was always the way yet they had tried to do things in their own way, they all had their own plans.

> *"My frame was not hidden from you when I was made in the secret place. When I was woven together in the depths of the earth, your eyes saw my unformed body. All the days ordained for me were written in your book before one of them came to be." Psalm 139: 14–16 (NIV)*

No matter what our plans, His plans will prevail, even when we manage to make wrong choices, take wrong roads, and really mess things up, God will make it all come out for His good, for His glory.

God Where Are You?

Tuesday morning came and it was a beautiful day for our plans. We got up early and had to drive about an hour to our first meeting. Idaho is an hour ahead of California so we were up early, had our free breakfast at the hotel and we were on the road to accomplishing our plans. At around 9:15 A.M. Idaho time we received a call on the cell phone. Larry Sr. was very upset and wanted to know if we were ok.

"Of course we're ok, what's wrong?" His reply we were not ready for.

"I got this horrible phone call and I thought it was you. Listen and see what you think."

My heart fell as I listened. I knew immediately something terrible had happened. The screams were coming from Larry's ex-wife Heather. The sounds I heard were those of someone beyond hysterical: guttural screams, un-earthly screams.

"That's Heather, something is terribly wrong," I said.

I turned to Larry, his first words were, "The kids are hurt, they have been in an accident, the kids are hurt, and I have to call Heather."

I told Larry Sr. I would call him back and immediately called Heather's work. She had not arrived and no one knew why. We called our office and one of our employees, told me he had received a phone call earlier that morning and didn't know who it was and that the woman kept saying "your daughter is dying."

He asked, "Where are you?"

The reply "I'm on Buena Vista."

He told her "Hang up and call 911." The phone call ended abruptly.

Later he described that morning and the call in detail. The call had come in a little before eight o'clock. One of our staff usually was in around that time and his first thought was something had happened to her, as he knew she took that road in the morning to take her daughter to day care. Another staff member came in and he shared his fears. They waited and as it happened that day the staff member was around 15 minutes late. They were thrilled and relieved when she walked in the door. He relayed the conversation to her and she immediately called Michelle. They all determined at that time the call must have been a wrong number.

Our next call was to my daughter Michelle. All of our grandchildren went to school together and she would know if Heidi and Haydon had shown up for school. I reached her on her cell phone. "Michelle, where are you?"

Michelle's response was, "Mom, there's been an accident; I am trying to get there. I called the school and they told me there had been an accident and Heidi and Haydon were not at school."

"Where is the accident?" I asked.

"Buena Vista, I'm there and trying to get down to a policeman."

Larry immediately took the phone. "Michelle, get to a policeman and get them on the phone."

"Larry, I'm trying to but they will not let me through," Michelle said.

"You have to get through, tell them the father is on

the phone."

Inside Michelle is frantic. Her thoughts and fears, what had happened to her beloved niece and nephew, to Heidi and Haydon?

"I have to get through, I have to find out where they are, are they hurt I have to help. I have to get to a policeman for Larry."

Several minutes go by before Michelle can finally reach a policeman that will talk to her.

This time is an eternity to us. I am sitting waiting, praying, "Dear God, please protect Heidi and Haydon, don't let anything happen to them."

Why is it taking so long to get to a policeman?

Larry is frantic; yelling on the phone to Michelle, "Get to someone, NOW!"

"I have the father on the phone, he is out of town on business, and you have to talk to him."

Policeman, "Who am I speaking to?"

"Larry Nix, I am the father. What happened?"

While speaking with Larry the policeman walked off out of earshot of Michelle. She is standing there waiting to find out something, anything. Where are the kids, are they ok?

"Is Heather your wife?"

"No, she is my ex-wife, what happened?"

"Are you alone?"

"No, I am in Idaho on business. I am with my Mother. Tell me what happened are my kids ok?"

As Larry was speaking I continued praying, continued pleading with God. "God please let these children be safe. God please do not let them be hurt."

Policeman: "There has been an accident, your son was taken to Western Medical with minor injuries, he will be fine. Your ex-wife also went to Western Medical with injuries. Your daughter died in transit to Placentia Linda Hospital."

Larry turned to me with a look of total shock and disbelief, his face white, drained of life.

"Mom, Heidi is dead, Mom, my little girl is gone."

All feeling left my body, a defining moment of no return, a direction change in all of our lives, Larry's life, and his future taken away in an instant.

"God, no, no!" That's all I could say, instant numb, shock beyond human understanding.

I could only keep thinking of Gods words *"Never will I leave you; never will I forsake you." Hebrews 13:5b (NIV)*

"God you promised not to leave me. Where are you now?"

Oh God. . . . No

The policeman continued to ask Larry questions, he could not think, he handed the phone over to me. He was asking phone numbers and addresses. I told him Michelle was my daughter and could answer any question he needed. He told me not to let Larry drive. I asked him to give the phone back to my daughter.

In my heart I was continuing to pray, "God help this family, we need your protection, help us. I don't know what to do, direct us, guide us, and help us. God, NO, NO!"

"Michelle."

"Mom, what's wrong?"

"Michelle, Heidi has been killed."

"No, oh no." Her knees went weak and she had to sit down on the curb.

"Michelle, you have to get to Haydon. You have to stay with him until we can get home. Larry does not want him to be alone. He will be so frightened. He is at Western Medical, take your Dad and go, and get there as soon as you can. Call me back when you get there."

I could hardly make out her response through the deep sobs the thick emotions, "Ok."

My next call was to my husband, Larry Sr.

Larry Sr. later told me as he was driving to the accident he was struck by the awful feeling that Heidi had died. He could not explain the feelings but he was overcome by deep emotion and physical pain. God was preparing him.

"Larry, where are you?"

"I'm driving to the accident, I need to get there."

"Larry, pull over."

"I have to get there."

"Larry, pull over now." A few minutes passed.

"OK, I'm stopped."

"Heidi is dead; she was killed in the accident."

"Oh my God no, oh God no." I could hear the emotions boil up and prayed he could hold together for Haydon.

"You need to get to Haydon, you have to stay with him he'll be very scared."

"OK, OK, Oh God, my Heidi."

I called Michelle back, "Michelle, call Dave at church, we need to get in touch with Dave."

"OK."

Ripples from the Stone

Dave Higgins, a dear friend, a member of our Life Group and one of the pastors at our church, he needed to know in order to help us. How he would help us I did not know, I just knew he would get everyone together and start praying for us.

Michelle hung the phone up and called our office. She rattled off instructions, one of them being "Call Dave at our church."

The police had stopped Larry Sr. from driving up to the accident. He had parked his truck and walked the few blocks to get to Michelle. Tony, Michelle's husband, could not get to where they were as the street was closed off. Michelle reached him on the cell phone and had him meet them at home. With tearful embracing and shaking Michelle and her Dad somehow managed to walk back to their cars and drive to Michelle's house. They picked up Tony and all drove to Western Medical to get to Haydon not knowing what they would find.

As they ran into the hospital they were met by our friend Judy who had come to the hospital in order to give support to our family. The office staff had been notifying friends and family of the horrible accident. The hospital allowed Michelle and Tony to go into the room with Haydon as no other family member was there. This little boy sat stoic and quiet, alone and terrified. He held on to his Aunt Michelle with his wide eyes filled with fear. While Michelle and Tony were in with Haydon, Heather's parents came up to Larry Sr. in the lobby. Patty, Heather's mother, asked Larry Sr. what had happened.

He said, "There's been an accident. Heather and Haydon are ok, but Heidi was killed."

Patty's knees went weak and he helped her sit down as Will, Heather's stepfather, came up to hear the news. Larry Sr. thought Patty and Will already knew what had happened. It upset him terribly to be the one to tell them of Heidi's death. Shortly thereafter Heather's sister, Ashley, entered the hospital and was told about the accident and Heidi's death. Ashley was so very close to Heidi and it was a devastating blow to her. How they all loved Heidi. Ashley was such a wonderful influence on this little angel. Ashley shared her love of Jesus with Heidi and was a positive influence in her life.

Michelle, Tony and Larry Sr. came out with Haydon and took him around the back way so he would not have to see the brokenness of his other grandparents, aunt and uncle. Their focus was to get to Heather and help her through this ordeal. They knew Haydon would be ok, as they had been told he was going home with Michelle.

Around lunchtime, Michelle picked her children up from school not wanting them to hear about Heidi's death from anyone else. Heidi's teacher, shaken to her soul, had left school on hearing the news. She had heard there was a car accident and when school started and the only empty seat was Heidi's, her heart fell with such weight she had to leave. This tragedy had a ripple effect on so many. As the stone was thrown into the waters of life the ripples began. God's hand was moving, and lives were being changed.

Seeing with God's Eyes

Numb and Shattered

Larry and I sat for a moment in shock. We got out of the car, crying, and hugged each other. Feeling total disbelief, Larry's heart was crushed, so lost, and so empty. Not really knowing what to do just feeling numb. We knew we had to get home and our minds focused on that task, not being able to comprehend the reality of what we had just heard. Only God could help us now, we had no strength. I kept telling myself this is not real. God how could this happen? Make this not real. We sat numb and completely shattered.

Larry and I started driving to the airport. I think it was our first instinct in our fight or flight mentality. I truly believe the Holy Spirit was directing our steps, He was in total control, and we were in His plan. The first thing He did was slow us down. We had to start taking things one-step at a time. The first step was to get a flight out of Utah and back home.

My first call was to Southwest Airlines to see if we could get on an earlier flight; it was around 10:00 in the morning Idaho time. My cell phone had not charged the night before and I just kept praying it would hold out until we got home.

Southwest:

"We have a flight at 11:00 A.M."

"Great, book us on that, we are about 2 hours from the airport, I hope we can make it."

Larry wanted to drive and I let him. He told me

he had to do something. "As long as you stay under 100 mph you can drive."

Have you ever been to Idaho or northern Utah? There is never traffic, open roads. Well, not this day. Trucks passing trucks, construction, and motor homes in both lanes, every thing that could slow us down did.

"Mom, I think God is trying to slow us down."

"Larry, I think so too, we are on His time now not ours."

We talked, cried, and cried more. We were operating in survival mode now. No time for too much emotion, we had to get home. Again, the Holy Spirit was there to keep us numb yet moving in the right direction. Too much to think about, had to just get to the airport.

"Mom, I always wanted Heidi to know I fought for her through the divorce to have more time with her, to get her into a good school, she was so important to me. I fought for everything good in her life. One day I knew she would know and now . . . . . ." he fell into deep sobs.

"Larry, Heidi knew and she knows now. She now sees as God sees, from the beginning to the end and she knows how deep your love is for her and that you fought for her."

Larry spoke with a shaky voice, "You know what the last thing I did with Heidi? I prayed with her. On Friday morning I took her to school. We got there a little early and we read a book and then we said a prayer. My daughter is gone."

He had to stay focused on driving but the emotions were coming out with no control.

Angel from Heaven

He kept talking, remembering, "Wednesday morning Heidi told me she prayed to God and asked Him to take her to heaven. I told her I hope not yet; she had a lot to do in her life. Do you think she knew?"

How do you answer that? Did I think she knew? I believe children have a deeper sense within about life. The world teaches them to suppress this inner connection to God; they learn most people don't want to know these deep inner thoughts, the thoughts of a child in their innocence shared with God. Heidi was such a loving little girl. Her Heidi hugs were wonderful, loving and full of life. She was the most giving and un-selfish of all the grandchildren. She would give you anything you wanted of hers. She would share without a word. A special child with special insight into God's ways, Larry Sr. had always called her his "angel from heaven."

God, Please Help Us

Dave Higgins reached me on my cell phone, "I will stay with your family, Marsha this is going to be really big for your family, I will be there, and you are all in our prayers. Be safe getting home."

Really big for our family was an understatement. The depth of this cut has caused pain in every part of our life. The raw emotions, the fear that has been exposed and how each person has or has not dealt with it, to this day, pours out like a stuck artery and continues bleeding. No closure, no stopping the flood of emotions. The cut has hit every miss-placed feeling, every stuffed down hurt and brought it out like the ooze of pus from an infected wound: ugly, dirty, brutal and raw.

We arrived at the airport at 11:05 A.M., we missed our flight. Dropped the car off and ran in to see when the next available flight was: 6 P.M.

I was screaming: "No, we have to get home earlier, you don't understand my granddaughter has been killed we have to get home."

Everyone staring at us with a blank glazed look, like I was speaking a foreign language, I could feel the panic setting in. "God Help us!"

I could not let my mind go too far, we had to find a flight home, just get a flight home.

Again the Holy Spirit stepped in, "Keep moving down the line, stay calm, stay numb."

As I went down the line of ticket counters, Larry stood back against the wall, sobbing in disbelief. Asking at every airline, can you get us into Orange County or Ontario, how soon? There were no flights out. At the last counter I asked about a charter flight; not from this airport. We would have to take a cab to another airport and hire a charter. I stopped and asked God for help. "What do I do?"

His answer: "Stop . . . Wait."

At that moment a women from the Southwest ticket counter came running down the line.

"I can get you into LAX, it leaves at 2 P.M., and you will land around 3 P.M. California time. Do you want it?"

I looked at Larry. "Yes, Yes, book us."

Waiting Rooms

The wait for the flight was very difficult. Waits are always difficult. In the waiting rooms of life we spend so many dark hours. If you have not experienced those times it is hard for you to comprehend how difficult they are and how lonely you feel. In time everyone has a waiting room experience. I have waited for my mother to come out from surgery to hear a doctor say, "Its breast cancer." I have waited for the doctor to come out and tell us, "Your dad needs bypass surgery." I waited for a doctor to tell me my husband is a diabetic and will have to take insulin shots for the rest of his life. I have sat and listened as a doctor tells me my mother is terminal and waited 13 days for her to die in our home. I have listened to a doctor tell me my father had leukemia after surviving a second bypass operation and dying on the operating table, only to survive that close call and die a year later. I have waited for the doctors to tell us that Haydon's surgery was a success and he did not lose the use of his tongue or shoulders and it was not a tumor but a cyst. I waited for my son to come out from routine knee surgery to be faced with life threatening high blood pressure. I have waited for a phone call from the doctor to tell me my thyroid tumor was malignant and further surgery and radiation would be necessary. Today I wait for the healing of our family that has been torn apart with grief, fear and anger. I could go on and on about waiting and being in God's waiting rooms. Yet, some of God's best work is done in waiting rooms.

    Your faith is never tested more than in those lonely dark places. I have never felt alone, just lonely in my own thoughts and feelings. There may be many people sitting with you and holding your hand yet you must go through the valley, wait in the desert or walk in the shadow of death by yourself with God. You must trust him completely to see you through no matter the outcome. It is at these times you learn how deep your faith and trust truly are. It is at these most deep and dark times when the fog comes over you like thick mud; it is during these times of waiting that you grow in wisdom and in faith. It is during these times you learn what it is to trust God completely.

> *"And the Peace of God, which transcends all understanding, will guard your hearts and your minds in Christ Jesus." Philippians 4:7 (NIV)*

This wait was one of those times. I was never more confident that God had placed me here with Larry for a purpose, yet I knew this was a road he was going to have to walk alone with God as his helper, not me. I knew in the depth of my heart it would be a difficult journey for the entire family. I just wanted to sit down and cry, scream, anything but wait in an airport full of little girls and people that were walking around like nothing had happened. Didn't they know my granddaughter had died, been killed, that Heidi was gone? No, I cannot let my mind go there; we just have to get home. Just get on the plane, that's all we have to do. Put my feelings aside, I can feel later.

God, Please Lift This Burden

Larry and I talked a lot and we sat and prayed for strength to just get home. "God please be with our family, with Haydon."

"Mom, I should be there, Haydon needs me."

"Haydon is safe, you will be there soon, and he knows you're on the way home." I wanted my words to give him some type of relief but I knew they didn't, how could they?

Michelle had called and they had Haydon home

with the other kids. Our family had to sit and wait for us to get home. They were also in a waiting room, a room of shock, fear, and extreme sadness. They made calls to other friends and family members. How do you share such a tragedy when you have such a broken heart? The words can hardly come out of your mouth. The echo of each word seems to make no sense; it is just a sound, a clanging noise.

Unknown to us, several of our friends and clients had seen the accident on the morning news. Some had seen it on their computers as pop up news. Shock overtook many, and they had to leave work, too broken to continue. The stories of how each person learned of Heidi's death would touch us for many months to come.

The next call was to let Michelle know when we would be coming in. I could not remember the flight number all I could tell her was the time and airline. Michelle had our staff check on the Internet to see what the flight number was and arranged to have our friends be there to pick us up. Our friends Judy and Larry wanted desperately to be the ones to come and pick us up. They felt it would be better for them to be there as they both wanted to hold us and pray with us. We were so glad to see them and knew they had been in continual prayer since learning of this tragedy.

"Mom, they want someone to identify the body." Michelle spoke with such sadness in her voice barely able to get the words out.

"Michelle, your Dad won't be able to do that. Will they wait until Larry gets there? No, Larry can't do that."

"No, Tony will have to go."

Tony, Michelle's husband, the most un-emotional person in the family was now out of control. His emotions were rushing every which way. The fear of having to identify the torn body of a little girl that he loved, how would he handle this? The emotions that Tony would go through and never deal with would eventually create a devastating result in his marriage to Michelle. Grief has a way of destroying even the strongest ties and their ties were already strained. The drop of so many tears can eat through and corrode anything. The salt will destroy and the rust will eat through the lives that grief has touched. Tony would end up running away from the hard work it takes to work through grief, to work through life. Just wanting to be "happy" again, Tony never learned to lean on God. So many times when you are "self-made" you only lean on self. When God decides to bring you into His plan He will get you there one way or another. If you continually resist, I believe God lets you go. God never gives up, He just lets you take your own road putting people in your path to give you the opportunity to choose Him again and again until one day it is too late. And so it was with Tony leaving Michelle and his four beautiful blessings.

Tony agreed he would do the body identification not really understanding how out of control he was. Dave, on the other hand, knew this would not be something Tony could handle on his own, if at all. So Dave began praying. "God if at all possible please lift this burden from Tony, don't put him through this. Intercede and remove this heavy load."

Dave drove to the hospital with Tony, praying all the way. When they walked in the front door Tony told Dave he was having great difficulty and was not sure he could do this. When they entered the hospital they were met by a staff member who informed them, "You do not have to identify the body." Dave's prayer was answered.

This gave Tony an opportunity to be thankful for God's intervention. However, to be thankful for God's hand at work in your life you must know God.

At that time we did not know that no one would be able to see Heidi's body again. It was not viewable. The damage to this little girl was beyond the ability of a loving father to understand. This has been one of the hardest parts of loosing Heidi. Not being able to hold her hand and say goodbye, to *let* her go. She was *taken* without a goodbye kiss, without one last hug. Even when you understand that death is not the end, the separation from your loved one is sometimes beyond your ability to cope. When you lose a loved one and never see them or touch them, the reality of what has happened takes a long time to understand, to accept. You just know at any moment they will walk through the door and the nightmare will have been one big joke. I understood Heidi was with Jesus, I just wanted a chance to touch her one last time, to say "Goodbye, see you shortly, I love you."

Focus on the Gift

The Flight Home

Sitting and waiting at the airport allowed our minds to run wild with questions. Each time my mind would take off I would pull it back. Feel later, just get home. Each time Larry would start to question, start to cry, he would focus on getting home, we just need to get on the plane.

It's strange how survival mode works on your mind. This was such a shock to us we could, at some moment say, this was not happening. Here we are so far away, it is not real. Survival mode works great to get you through a tragedy, a crisis. However, you can get stuck there and we did. Not just for a few weeks, but for a year. All we focused on was just getting by. Get back to work and you'll feel better, find out what happened and you will understand, none of that works. It is just another way of stuffing down the pain, which turns to fear and then to anger, anger at anyone, everyone, the pain, so deep. The amputation is complete, yet you continue to bleed.

Finally, they started boarding. Oh, no we're one-way passengers; we will be pulled aside for the security check.

"Larry, I will take the computer, you get checked and get on, and I will follow."

"How is your day, Sir?" The usual question asked by the screeners.

"Not very well, I just found out my daughter has

been killed in a car accident and I am trying to get home to my son."

With a shocked look on his face, "I am so sorry, go on in."

The screener walked over to where they were going through the computer and was telling the second screener about what Larry had told him.

"Yes, that is my granddaughter, and that is my son. We are trying to get home." When they finished checking the computer I was allowed to board the plane.

The flight was not full which allowed Larry and me to have our own aisle. How God provided for us. Larry sat in front of me and would bow his head, and his shoulders would shake as he wept uncontrollably. My heart was breaking not only from losing Heidi but at seeing my son so shaken, shaken to his very foundation.

She Is Not Lost

Heidi was his life. He did everything for his children; they were his focus, his reason to exist. Larry and his two children had lived with us for 5 years. When Heidi was three, they moved in with us. She was so special to me words cannot express. They were planning on buying a home and would sit and look at magazines and pick out ways to decorate their new home. They would talk about their vacations, school, read together, pray together, cook together, and cuddle every night together. She was his every breath. He always said Heidi was his "Girlie girl." She was developing her own style and she loved the 60's and 70's look, bell-bottom pants, tie-dye tops, and all the bright colors. Yet, when her dad was traveling or they had a special day together, she loved to wear his t-shirts to bed. She always told me "I love to smell my Daddy in his shirts." I would tell her they were smelly and she would hold them up and tell me how good they smell, "Just like Daddy." How I longed to be able to hold her, smell her in her Daddy's t-shirt and stroke her curly blond hair.

When you lose a child you lose your future, your plans for life, the continuation of life itself. The loss of a child will change your life in ways no other loss can. Your very body will break down as the grief tears at its every fiber. It is not uncommon for family members to be diagnosed with cancer, heart disease and many other physical problems within a year or more of the child's death. As the grief tears at your body, your mind cannot function and you want desperately to escape reality. Job loss and business loss is a common occurrence when a child has died, your mind is not able to take on the extra burden of business, of thinking through daily problems that once was so easy. Larry had lost his Heidi girl, no, his daughter had been taken by a tragic automobile accident caused by a wrong choice. Larry knows where Heidi is, she is not lost; she is at *home*.

God's Gift

I believe you can only understand the depth of grief when you have gone through it and that your ability to "go there" with a parent that has lost a child can come only from your own experience of a child's death. Someone who has not gone through this grief cannot possibly come close to understanding. This is not to discount anyone's loss of a loved one, a job, your health or financial crises. Each person's experience with loss is difficult, heart wrenching and life changing. No one's loss is better or worse than another, each is just as painful, each is different, each is soul changing.

When you lose a grandchild you also lose a part of your child, a part of your future legacy is gone, a part of you will not continue, it is cut off, it is dead. Your child is the present and your grandchildren are your future. Grandchildren are a promise from God that in some small way you will continue on. Everyone has a desire to live forever and to know they made a difference. Just like Abraham and Sarah, their desire to leave a heritage, God had promised them a heritage and he did not fail at his promise, He never does. That is what a grandchild is, God's promise of seeing the end of the rainbow and the pot of gold. They fulfill the circle of life and each generation you add are blessings beyond measure. They are your showers of blessings, your mercy drops come to life.

Children come to us as blessings, as gifts that God gives us to rear and teach. It has taken me years to understand that we are not only to teach them not to run in front of cars or not to put their hand in a fire but above all we are to teach them of God's ways and plans for their life and in this I failed miserably with my own children. Our children were ego extensions of what we wanted from life and not until much later when they were older did I realize it was not about what I wanted for them but what God wanted from me and from them and for them. It was a process for me to understand the true blessings our children are and their life is just that, their life, given to me to nurture, guide and above all love. We may have the words to say how much we love and appreciate them but not until you lose a child do you really know how wide and how deep their lives have touched and changed your soul. When we lost Heidi it became clear to me, children are not a gift they are on loan to us. God gives them to us to enjoy, to love, to teach and then send them out on their own and sometimes He takes them *home*.

View Life Vertically

Our children have many hurts that were perpetuated by my view of life. Much of my life was being a self-made person, forcing relationships, making my children obey, and manipulating life so it would be my way. My children learned well to come to their parents for anything and everything they needed, we could fix it all. They should have learned, you go to God, He is the one in control, not your parents. I have come to understand that my view of life was horizontal. That is not God's plan for our life; we are to view life vertically, looking up to God for direction in everything, not just the big stuff but also the small stuff. If I "do it my way" and society thinks me successful, when "my way" goes bad what right do I have to cry out to God to help me? I took Him out of the picture. Only when I look up for direction and guidance and turn it over to God can I find the light in this dark desert.

My peace comes from knowing God will use even my mistakes to glorify Him, to guide my children, to restore our family in His time and His way. I must admit, however painful, I could have done a much better job rearing my children if I had allowed God to guide me sooner. Knowing the pain my children will have to go through in gaining the knowledge they should have received from their parents hurts beyond belief.

God knew what type of parent I would be and He knew our children would need to fight to break out of the cocoon that had been placed around them. As they struggle their strength increases, it is only when we, their parents, try to fix life for them and cut them out of the cocoon do they become weak. Just like a butterfly that receives its strength by struggling out of the cocoon, we all need the struggles in life to grow strong in our faith. It is during these difficult times we grow in our walk with Jesus and gain knowledge of our purpose here on earth.

Even with the hurts you have with children they some how bless you with grandchildren. If children are blessings, just think what GRAND children are.

"Children's children are a crown to the aged." Proverbs 17:16 (NIV)

They are truly grand, truly a "Crown of the aged." We are given another chance to love unconditionally and it seems to work better this time around. Our grandchildren love us even with our funny ways. They want to cook like Grandma or play tennis like Grandpa. Even when their parents, our children, shake their heads with disgust the grandchildren embrace us, and find our love and hug a welcome change to the demands of parents. As grandparents when we lose a grandchild we lose the unconditional love and acceptance of a child, the child that loves us in spite of their parent's actions and feelings toward us. We have a mutual unconditional love for each other.

Flying in the Clouds

The other side of losing a grandchild is the compounded pain of not being able to help your child. Compare it to standing and watching someone cut off an arm or leg of your child without anesthesia. They feel the pain directly and are expected to scream, cry, yell, be sick, be angry and lash out. You feel the pain and are expected to cry in private, hold everything around you together and be supportive. I was trying so hard to hold everything around me together as I watched the knife silently cut the flesh and bone of my son.

"Mom, I think it appropriate I am flying in these clouds today." Larry remarked as the plane flew high into the beautiful white clouds.

"I think so too. You know God put us here together on this trip for a reason, now we know what that reason is."

The Apprehension of Home

As we approached LAX, Larry got up to go to the restroom. The flight attendant asked if he was ok and he told her what had happened. As her eyes filled with tears, she told him they would let us off first, a kindness that touched our hearts. We would not have to stand with tears streaming down our cheeks and face the quizzical stares of onlookers, of strangers.

As the plane landed the apprehension was building. We made it home but what do we do now? Charles Swindoll describes apprehension as "The pillow we put over our faith."

In my mind all I could think of was the leading of the Holy Spirit: "Trust God, he will lead you through this."

We de-planed and were met by loving Christian friends with open arms and tearstained faces. Not knowing what to say they held on to us and shared in our shock. I went and got our luggage as Larry went to the car with our friends. This was just the beginning of the journey. Little did we know our trip back would be the easiest part for now we were home and had to face the reality of this tragedy. Our landing began a long string of heart wrenching experiences, times of deep depression, and a journey to the center of our souls.

Our friends did not know that we were unaware of how the accident had happened. We had talked of the possibilities, but none came close to what would eventually be found out. Larry was told that his ex-wife had slammed into the back of a stopped truck that was making a left hand turn. That Heidi's body was still at Placentia Linda Hospital where she was pronounced dead. At that time there were no concerns of what really happened it was just about Heidi and Haydon. Larry knew the coroner would pick up the body; he wanted someone he knew to be with her if he could not. Larry's first thoughts, call Beth.

Everyone in Their Place

One Last Touch

"Mom, call Beth at the coroners office, I do not want Heidi to have an autopsy performed on her. I just want to make sure they don't do that, there is no need."

Larry had dated Beth in high school and had reconnected with her shortly after his divorce. Beth had since remarried and they had not spoken in a couple of years. When God has a plan for your life, He makes sure everyone is in his or her place. As you read this story you can look back over the years and see how people being in or at a special place in your life made a difference. So many times we say how lucky we were so and so happened to be there, or how lucky we were such and such happened at that time. This is not luck; it is Gods plan for your life.

> "Many are the plans in a man's heart, but it is the Lord's purpose that prevails." Proverbs 19:13 (NIV)

How do you call someone you know, someone who at one time loved Larry and tell her not only that Heidi had died but she would have her body there at the coroner's office?

Having been connected to the coroner's office from a 411 call I heard Beth's voice.

"Beth, this is Marsha, I need to ask a special favor

of you." I was not sure if she had heard the news or not.

"Hi Marsha, sure anything." From the sound of her voice I knew she did not know the purpose of the call.

Beth told me later that she had expected me to tell her my husband had died and I wanted her to handle his body.

"Larry's little girl Heidi was killed in a car accident this morning . . ."

"Oh God, is she at Placentia Linda?"

"Yes, why?"

"I was called to take that pick up but someone else was closer so I did not go. She must be the 6 year old they called about."

"Heidi was 8."

"Maybe they made a mistake. I will check on it and find out. How is Larry doing, oh what a stupid question. What do you need me to do?"

Her comment *"made a mistake"* would become prophesy of the entire investigation. Larry would find mistake after mistake made by shoddy investigators, police that ignored procedure and fireman so shaken by the scene that they did not report the complete accident. To this day those mistakes have not been corrected.

"Beth, Larry does not want an autopsy done on Heidi."

"Let me find out some more details and I will call you back. Tell Larry I will call him. I am so very sorry." Her voice quaking as she hung up.

Beth would be the last person to touch Heidi's little hand. The body was not picked up and brought to the coroner's office until later that afternoon. When Beth found out all the information she called back and the news was not something Larry wanted to hear. They were going to do an autopsy on Heidi because the police were going to do an investigation. This is standard procedure when a death occurs in a car accident. This devastated Larry even more. He knew what they did in autopsies, he had toured the coroners office and been told in detail. Beth assured him she would take care of everything. However, once the coroner found out Beth knew our family, they would not allow her to be involved in the autopsy. They would not even allow her to see the pictures, as they were so gruesome. Once the autopsy was completed, Heidi's little body was laying covered up on the table. Beth walked by and Heidi's little hand was hanging out from under the cover. She took her hand and gently tucked it back under the sheet. How very much we envied that last touch of our precious Heidi.

Embraced By God

The drive home from the airport seemed endless. The traffic was unusually heavy that day, or so it seemed. Everything was moving in slow motion. This had to be a horrible dream. The reality of this tragedy was so overwhelming, its thickness was like a shield and nothing could sink in. How does Larry tell Haydon his sister is dead? At this point Larry had no idea what Haydon had seen or experienced. As time passed Haydon would share with Larry what Heidi looked like and how he knew she was dead as he sat next to her in the car. It would be months before Haydon could share how the accident happened. Larry's ability to allow Haydon the freedom to talk and share this horrible experience has been helpful and healing to both of them.

How do you tell these children that are so very close that their cousin is in heaven and we will not see her on earth any more? Where do you start? You start by praying. "God if you can lift this horrible event from our life please do so. If you can make any sense of this please start now. How will we ever get through this? How will you make something good come from this tragic loss? God, where are you? I need you now; please do not leave us in this our darkest hour. Guide us in our words to these children."

We pulled into the driveway and everyone came out to meet us. We all grabbed each other and cried, and I prayed, "God give us strength and wisdom as we talk to these little children. Protect them and hold us up as a family."

Dave was there waiting. He had not left the family's side. He had been with Tony praying for protection. He had been with Michelle and Larry Sr. talking and praying with them. Larry and I were told that the kids knew about Heidi's death. Michelle and Tony had told them when they picked them up from school. Larry immediately ran out to Haydon. He needed to be with his son, to make sure he was ok. They clung to each other tightly not wanting to let go. They cried and held each other. His now, only child, was the most important person in his life. Heidi was his strength, his reason to live. He often said she made him a better man. Larry could have pulled away from Haydon out of fear of being hurt but he embraced this little boy who had been the witness to the brutal death of his sister. This little boy needed his dad more than ever and they both needed God to embrace them. Together they reached up and God reached down and He continues to hold them through this tragedy, through this long on-going journey.

A Time to Cry

That Tuesday became an image in my mind that would never leave. The days that followed became a blur and it was only by guidance and strength of the Holy Spirit that came to us through friends and family that we made it. When we finally got home that night the phone messages were non-stop. Yet as I walked into the house, a house where Heidi had lived for 5 years, a house that had her bedroom full of her clothes still there, it seemed so different. I immediately felt God's presence and knew He had placed a protection around our house, a protection of the Holy Spirit. We could cry, wail, scream, get mad, and God would hear us and wipe our tears away. Oh, the tears that would fall without stopping, tears that could fill a lake, an ocean, as the emotions came crashing down on each one of us. Tears of grief so unending, so deep, that you would literally hurt physically. We had only gone through the first day of this journey and felt as if it had been a lifetime.

Our Life Group from church called and wanted to come over and be with us. We had joined a Life Group a few years earlier. This is a small group of Christian friends that come together once a week to share life with, to study God's word and support each other on our daily walks. They were, and are family to me, each one a blessing in my life, a blessing beyond words. This was another place God had put us to prepare us for this time. He knew we would need their love and support, their wisdom, their helping hands through this tragedy. I cannot express the over-whelming feeling of God's love that I felt that evening. Even today we continue on in this group supporting each other through the trials of life.

When you walk through the valleys and the journey is long it is so important to have people willing to board the train and travel with you. They may not be able, nor is it their place to *fix* everything for you, but to know you have someone to lean on and pray with and love you no matter what happens, is necessary in your healing. Just remember, someone may extend a helping, loving hand but you must accept that hand of grace. As Jesus extends His hand of grace to us it is our choice to accept His gift of salvation, so it is with those around you in times of grief. Their hand extended, I reached up and held on tightly. They became my connection to hope that life would go on someday.

Larry wanted to be with Haydon, to hold him and not let him out of his sight. As our group gathered I made the first of many mistakes. I say *mistakes* but I am not sure in any situation like this there are rights and wrongs. As Larry Sr. and my heart was breaking we sometimes forgot a large part of Larry's heart was now gone. A hole was now in his heart so big only God can fill it. I tried so hard to stay focused on him but there were times the emotions would overcome me and I would slip away. He was the one whose arm and leg had been cut off. He was bleeding so badly. As our support group was gathering, Larry was holding on to his little boy who had seen more than many war veterans had seen in their entire career. I did not even think that he needed a break to go and cry, to be alone and to have someone else be with Haydon. After everyone left, Larry told me in a quiet, broken voice, "Please do not do that to me again. I need time to break down without Haydon there." He was asking, "Please help me. I have no strength, I need yours, and I need God's."

Unwanted Journey

Michelle and Tony had gotten up for a usual workday. It was also their fourteenth wedding anniversary. Getting four children dressed, fed and ready for their various schools and day care was always a challenge and this morning was no different. Tony left with Torey, their youngest daughter to take her to day care as Michelle left with Dylan 10, Hayley 8, and Colin 4 to take them to school where they would meet up with their cousins, Heidi and Haydon. Larry and I had started our day with scheduled sales meetings and a beautiful day to come home. Larry Sr. had started his morning excited about picking up Haydon and Heidi and looking forward to my arrival back home. In an instant, a wrong choice was made and God took Heidi *home* to be with him and our family's life changed forever. Many lives would never be the same no matter how much I prayed or cried or how much any of us hurt. We were all put on an unexpected, unwanted journey.

Taking the High Road

Planning a funeral is difficult at its best. I had planned three previous funerals, my husband's father, my mother and my father. Whenever a funeral is for someone you love deeply it carries such emotion and being able to focus becomes more difficult. I remember planning my mother's funeral, the most difficult of all before this, and picking out the clothes she would wear, picking out the flowers and music, the person to do the service. Planning the funeral for an 8-year-old little girl was heart wrenching. If it was heart wrenching for me it was beyond devastating to Larry. Again, I believe the presence of God was what kept us going as His hand kept us in a state of shock, in survival mode so we could take the steps necessary to continue.

The day after the accident Larry wanted to take Haydon to see his mother so he would know she was ok. Haydon who had shared parts of the horrific scene of the accident with Larry was also in shock and needed to feel reassured his mother was ok. Haydon had told us that immediately after the accident he was screaming for someone to get him out of the car. He recounted how he had unbuckled his seat belt but could not get the door open and how a man came and got him out of the car. I am sure he sat listening to his mother scream in horror knowing Heidi was not moving or speaking, knowing his sister was dead. Over the past months, Haydon has shared the stories of what happened, in gruesome detail, too much for a small boy to understand, too much for any of us to understand.

Larry Sr., Larry, Haydon and I walked into Western Medical and asked to see Heather. We were immediately escorted into a room off of the main waiting area. I can only imagine what the staff thought as they looked at us with our tear-stained faces, disheveled dress, beaten down posture and sleepless eyes. I am not sure they could even understand how difficult it was to be there. Larry was taking the high road as he had done so many times before when it came to his children. To our shock, we were informed none of us could go in to see Heather until we all met with a grief counselor.

We were escorted into a room full of toys and books and were questioned by a lady that, in hindsight, was not there just for our grief but also as crisis intervention to establish whether Larry was mentally capable and stable enough to see his ex-wife and not upset her. Later on, we were told by the hospital staff that Heather was fearful Larry might be violent when he found out she was driving the car when Heidi was killed. How wrong she was. Was Larry angry? Oh yes, yet his focus was on Haydon, always on Haydon, not on Haydon's mother. Larry always took the high road when it came to his children. His other focus that day, besides calming Haydon, was on planning Heidi's funeral and he wanted it to be all about Heidi. There would be time later to deal with his anger. We met with the counselor for over an hour before they allowed Larry and Haydon in to visit. This was a long, blurry hour of which I could hardly tell you what the counselor talked about. We all sat there like mannequins, talking like robots, not feeling anything. Feeling was not allowed at this point. Just keep moving.

The Un-imaginable Weight

Larry and Haydon were allowed to see Heather and it gave both Haydon and his mother a sense of relief. Once Larry was with Heather alone, they talked about their desires for handling Heidi's funeral. Heather and her family wanted to cremate Heidi and throw her ashes out over the ocean. They had never had a funeral, they had never known what it was to say goodbye and grieve a loved one. Larry was adamant about having a funeral and burying Heidi. He had the foresight to know someday Haydon would want a place to go and mourn his sister. Heather told him to do whatever he wanted; there would be no argument. That was out of character for Heather not to stand and fight for her desires yet, I believe, it was probably her feelings of guilt that allowed her to give Larry that gift.

After a short while, Larry Sr. and I were allowed

to join them. Heather's sister and her husband along with Heather's boyfriend and a minister from her sister's church were waiting outside her door. Larry Sr. and I went in to see Heather and we each gave her a hug and told her how sorry we were. I could hardly believe the lack of emotion, she was so stoic. At the time I did not realize she was also in shock, numb, and in deep depression. Our survival mode did not allow us any compassion for someone else. That would have required the ability to think, to feel. It was hard for us to get through the day and we kept putting our feelings on the back burner.

For Heather it had to be emotionally unbearable. Denial would be the only way to handle this reality, at least for now. She had suffered a compound fracture to her arm and a fractured eye socket. The depth of her loss was unbelievable and depression would set in and show its dark head quickly. To have been the reason your child was killed is a weight I cannot imagine how you carry. That burden is something you must give to God or it will weigh you down and bury you. As she was put on suicide watch for a few days, I am sure the prayers of her family and friends held her in God's care.

Heather's mother and stepfather were not around. From that day on her stepfather, to my knowledge, has never spoken to Larry and has never shown compassion for Larry's loss, sadness and grief. He has acted out in anger and reproof of Larry. You would think Larry was the one who was driving the car. To this day I do not understand his attitude, his reproof and indifference. I believe he is so angry with Heather and cannot express this to her, so he has misdirected it to Larry. He spoke at Heidi's memorial service of the love he had for Heidi, he hugged me and cried, yet has never been able to share that with Larry. I can say not everything is for us to understand, that God moves in everyone's life differently. Our free will gets in the way sometimes but God's plans will ultimately come to pass. What a blessing this man has missed by not talking to Larry and not being able to share his feelings about this tragedy. Misplaced anger is something I have learned is common in the loss of a child. We all grieve differently; some reach for denial and bury their feelings, others grab every strand of emotion embracing their feelings.

Clothed in Glory, Covered in Fear

Planning a Funeral

We left the hospital, went home, had something to eat, and then Larry and I were off to the mortuary. Dave met us there to be the steady force for us. He brought us back when we could not think straight. His guidance and loving kindness were a blessing beyond measure. We had been told Heidi's body would be brought there the next day so we had to decide on a coffin. To even say her name and coffin in the same breath was so unthinkable. I remember driving up and parking the car, feeling as if I were having an out-of-body experience as we went in, filled out the paperwork and sat numb at a table while a man put pictures and prices in front of us.

Larry had never walked the path of planning a funeral and at his young age with young children, that was not uncommon. I looked back over the years and knew that was why I was with Larry. I had been through this with my parents and knew I could help him, guide him in what he would need. Larry picked out a beautiful casket, a spray of spring flowers that Heidi would love and then had to decide on a date and time for the funeral. As Heather was still in the hospital we knew it would not be before the following week. The accident happened on Tuesday April 29, 2003 and here we were on Wednesday trying to decide when Heather would be out of the hospital and plan a day that would work for everyone. Larry had been told Heather would probably be out of the hospital by Friday, May 2nd but would not be in any shape to go to a funeral on Saturday. With Dave's help, we decided on the following Saturday, May 10th, the day before Mother's Day. How interesting, if we had planned it on May 9th that would have been the day Larry and Heather were married ten years earlier. Again, with Dave directing us, we decided to have a private graveside early in the morning and a Memorial Service for Heidi at 11 A.M. at our church. We knew there would be many children attending and we wanted this to be a wonderful day in memory of Heidi. This would be a time to celebrate all of the events that would never happen; her graduations, prom, and wedding rolled into one day. At some point during the conversation we talked about how much this was going to cost. Larry didn't care, as he would find a way to pay for it, I just put it on my credit card and we moved on.

The part that stands out in my mind the most is when we talked about what to dress Heidi in. Larry chose to put no clothes on her. Her little body had been mutilated by the accident and what the accident did not do to her, the autopsy finished. When Larry made that decision my first thoughts were God's word

"Naked a man comes from his Mother's womb, and as he comes, so he departs." Ecclesiastes 5:15 (NIV)

"Now we know that if the earthly (body) tent we live in is destroyed, we have a building (new body) from God, an eternal house in heaven, not built by human hands. Meanwhile we groan, longing to be clothed with our heavenly dwelling, because when we are clothed, we will not be found naked. . .Therefore we are always confident and

> *know that as long as we are at home in the body we are away from the Lord." 2 Corinthians 5:1–6 (NIV)*

I knew Heidi was at *home* clothed in her new body, clothed in glory.

Provisions by God

That Wednesday evening our home was filled with friends, food, tears and a small surprise. The evening progressed and people were leaving around 10 or 11 P.M. We found the more tired we were, the easier it was to sleep for a short time. We had all gone over our experiences to the point of exhaustion. All of the kids were playing out of control or so it seemed. They did not understand any of this and it was especially hard on Haydon for he only knew his Dad was not spending much time with him and all he saw was people crying. Each time the doorbell would ring, he would ask, "Do I know them or do they know me?" Each night was a reoccurring event of food, friends and tears. My brother Tom and his wife Sandy had been out of town and came over as soon as their son had been able to get in touch with them. Sandy pulled me aside.

"I don't know if this is the time or not but I need to let you know there is a life insurance policy on Heidi. Tom took it out last year so he could win a trip. Do you remember us coming over to have Larry sign it?"

I did remember, but had forgotten and I was sure Larry did not remember.

"Yes I remember, and yes this is the time to tell us. I will let Larry know."

How prophetic that was.

As we spoke the incident all came back to me.

Wanting to *do something* for Larry, my brother Tom had called and talked to him about life insurance for his children. He would take out a life insurance policy on both Heidi and Haydon and it would not cost Larry anything. It would give them both a $10,000 life insurance policy that they could keep and increase when they got older if they chose to do so. They were so young and since it was only a small amount of money Tom would just pay for it. I remembered thinking how nice that was of Tom. Larry had almost refused it but at the last minute consented; he listened to the promptings of the Holy Spirit. This had taken place less than a year prior to Heidi's death. Was God's hand working to set everything in its place ahead of time? He knew the road Larry was going to have to travel and wanted to help him. How hard it was to acknowledge that this was all part of God's plan.

Did He want Heidi to die at that time? No, I do not think so. Did He know a choice was going to be made that day that would cost Heidi her life? I have asked myself that question a thousand times. I believe God put a choice in Heather's life, He hoped she would make the right one but He knew she would not. I believe God knew Heidi would join Him in heaven that day, that Heidi would go *home.* God loves us so much, He arranged a place for all of us to be and had started preparing us well in advance. He put in place everything that we would need to get us through these first few days, weeks, months and years. God had everything in its place; we just needed to keep our eyes on Him. Yet in our hurt we took our eyes off of God and we decided we could make decisions without Him. Our family made wrong choices, mistakes that would cause deep hurt and take years to heal, mistakes that we are feeling the effects of today, mistakes that I believe God is using in each one of our lives to shape us for continuing in His purpose.

The insurance policy was one of those occurrences that was so out of the ordinary only God could have planned it. In life when we cry out to God for help, we need only to open our eyes, be patient, and wait. God's way will be the solution you would have never thought of, it will be the one you see and say, WOW. That is God's way, so He will receive the praise, the glory. The life insurance that paid for the funeral and Heidi's head stone was just that, WOW. Larry spared no expense, why should he, this was his last gift to his daughter Heidi.

Daddy and Daughter

Each day I was surprised to see the sun come up. I just knew the world would stop with the pain and grief that Larry was feeling, that we were all feeling. My son hurt, and I hurt for him and for me. Sometimes it was hard to know which was more painful, Larry's hurt and not being able to do anything about it, or my pain and all the confusion it brought. My pain was so deep; his pain had drilled a hole all the way through him and no matter how hard he tried the hole kept growing. At night the tears and wailing, "My little girl is dead, Mom, she is gone." And then he would break down in deep sobs, uncontrollable waves of tears and all I could do is hug him, cry with him and watch as Heidi's death cut out his heart, yet he kept breathing.

Through all of the tears we were still putting together a funeral. This had to be everything for Heidi. I was going through pictures of my precious granddaughter. I cried as I watched a video of Christmas when she was three. Here she was so alive with her brother and Daddy loving each gift as she opened it with the excitement only a child has and smiling so big for the camera. We had to do a video for the funeral; we had to show the world our little angel. I had to ask Larry, it was his decision, and his desires. Larry wanted this to be a celebration of Heidi's life, that was the most important function of the funeral, remembering Heidi. First we had to find a place to bury Heidi.

Thursday, Larry and I met Dave at a local cemetery. We had several friends buried there and it had been suggested that since it was close to the church we might consider it. We drove around the grounds with an employee of the cemetery and he pointed out different areas that were available. Your mind is just not ready for this, how do you select a place to bury a little girl? Nothing was looking like a place we could come back to and feel close to Heidi. Around the last corner was a place with trees and had a substantial amount of plots available. Larry said "This is the place; I want to bury Heidi here." He ended up purchasing two double internment plots. He wanted to know he would be with Heidi when he dies, his body would be next to hers, their souls joined together in eternity, Daddy and Daughter.

Touched By Friends

Thursday night brought another night of people. Our office staff came to give hugs and cry with us. Heidi was a part of everything we did. Many of the staff Heidi had drawn pictures of, and she always had a hug for anyone willing to accept one. We are close to our staff, as a small office we know just about everything there is to know about each other. They were so very loving at this time. They were doing everything they could to hold the business together.

The day of the accident they were lost as what to

do. Dave had gone by to let them share and talk. I think most of them were also suffering from the shock and fear of what was going to happen to the business, to their jobs. The day after the accident, they all came together for a meeting and they all decided they would each do whatever it took to keep the business going while we were off. They met each day for lunch to share feelings and fears. Each one of them went out of their comfort areas and did tasks that they may have never done.

Tony went in to work more than any of us, as that was his escape from the feelings. Michelle was home with the kids, as they were not attending school. Yet, she made sure to communicate with the office staff every day. They all wanted to come see us and share our sadness. In some way I think it was also reassuring to them, we were ok and would be back in time. I look back on that time and realize God had put each one of them there for this purpose. I am not even sure they understood how important they were to us in keeping the business going. Our customers helped, our prospects postponed projects, God's hand reached far and deep.

What would we do without friends? The tears came each day and each night, just no stopping the pain. Yet every day and evening our loving friends were there bringing food, hugs, and just being there to listen or hold us. I have heard it said: "friends are God's apology for our families." I don't know if that is true, I know friends are God's arms and feet and voice. Over the next few weeks we had both friends and family reach out to us. My brother Tom took Larry to buy a suit for the funeral. He was there almost every night and took care of food at our home the day of the funeral. Friends came every night, our Life Group brought dinner and spent time praying with us and loving us. Other friends brought breakfast and lunch wanting so much to help in any way they could. One dear friend came and answered the phone while we met with Dave about the funeral so we did not have interruptions. Another friend brought us a couple of pictures he had blown up of Heidi and Larry in an awesome hug

and another picture of Heidi and Hayley with dress up hats on in their most winsome pose. I love those pictures.

(Heidi on the left,
Hayley on the right)

Friends came just to sit and hold us while we cried, no words, just love. One of our precious friends had a daughter that sang professionally and she offered to sing at the service. Friends called every night if they could not be there. Friends' reaching out to all of us in so many ways it was amazing. People we had not heard from in years called and came by. Larry had friends he had not communicated with since high school call and come by to share his grief. Young men he had played sports with called to tell him of their distress. Everyone shared their sadness and disbelief. We shared our absolute shock and horror.

Unbearable Fear

Thursday came and went then Friday, the day Heather was coming home. A day we all felt extremely uneasy about. We were not sure she would be coming home until late Friday afternoon. The fear Larry began to feel was tremendous. As the time grew closer, Larry knew she would want to have Haydon come home to her. His anxiety grew and how I feared for his own safety. His life was Haydon; his survival depended on keeping Haydon close. Heather was not going to be able to care for Haydon for some time, as bed rest was her prescription. Who could help him, who could protect Haydon, where do you turn, what do you do? When placed in a situation of extreme anxiety and fear, pray and trust God, no matter what.

That is not what happened, Larry had been taught well to fix things on his own, so in desperation he went to see his attorney. Under their visitation agreement if either one of the parents could not care for the children due to injury or illness the other would get temporary custody until the injured party could return to full care. In the past, Heather had surgery and Larry cared for the children for the week of her recovery, why would this be any different? Guilt does crazy things to people especially when the death of your child is involved. Desperate measures for desperate times, when fear starts guiding your path. Michelle went with Larry to see the attorney; he wanted so much to do what was right for Haydon, just for a little while, just for this time, he wanted right to prevail. He felt a conversation with Heather was out of the question; their communication was bad on a good day, how would this be handled without an attorney?

The attorney said they would need to sign some

legal papers and to expedite the process she would just call Heather while Larry was there. Once she identified herself and began to talk, Heather panicked and hung up. Her fear that this accident could cause her to lose Haydon put her in attack mode. She turned and told her mother and sister that Larry was trying to take Haydon away from her. She immediately called the police and told them Larry was not releasing Haydon and was in breach of his visitation rights. Heather got her two brothers-in-law to drive her to our home. Michelle and I were on our way to drop papers off at the cemetery and received a call. "Come home now."

Larry had called to tell us that Heather was coming for Haydon and he was not going to let her have him. He might end up getting arrested. At the time, we did not know that Larry had sent Haydon upstairs with Larry Sr. Larry had instructed his Dad not to let anyone take Haydon, no matter what and at any cost. Larry Sr., operating in his own fear of losing his grandson, locked the bedroom door and put a baseball bat next to him. He was not going to let anyone take his beloved Haydon. He turned on a movie for Haydon in order to distract him. The emotion of the moment was overwhelming to this little boy and he immediately went to sleep. Peaceful sleep was a wonderful escape for this traumatized child. In the mean time, Heather arrived and a confrontation of words began between the two. When Michelle and I returned home the two brothers-in-law were standing outside waiting for Heather to come out with Haydon. In a short time after our arrival she did. I walked up to her and hugged her.

Heather: "Your son and I just can not communicate."

I responded, "Well, this is a hard time to try and start."

Immersed In Pain

Shortly after Heather left, the police arrived as she did not call and tell them they did not need to come. After all why would she want to stop the police from showing up? At this moment in her life she probably felt, the bigger the hassle for Larry the better, how sweet the taste of revenge. She had been dealing with the police and their questions and acquisitions why not let Larry have to deal with them?

I did not understand the attitudes of the police officers and now with everything I have found out, I do not trust all of their motives. When the police arrived at our door, they wanted to know if the children were still here.

I replied, "No, the mother took the son."

Larry spoke up from the back with hurt and pain in his voice.

"What the *'expletive'* do you care, she killed my daughter and then you let her take my son."

One of the policemen turned and walked away, the other in his ignorance and arrogance, tried to intimidate Larry.

"What did you say? You don't need to mouth off to us."

I stepped in and told the policeman that Larry's daughter had been killed in a car accident with his ex-wife driving, yet he would not back off. The other policeman told him

"Let's go."

Larry in tears, fearful and on the edge, "Get the *'expletive'* out of here. You don't care."

Policeman: "Listen buddy, you don't have to take your anger out on us."

The other policeman saying "Let's go, leave it, sorry for your loss."

They both finally walk away. They drove down the street and parked their car for an hour to intimidate, just to make sure.

Little did they know or even care what had happened and no one could have made Larry feel anything at that point. He was totally immersed in pain and fear that was coming to rage. Larry had contacted his attorney about what he should do as Heather stood at the door. She advised him to let Haydon go, that he did not want to end up in jail that evening, as that would not help Haydon. Upon Larry instructing his dad to bring Haydon downstairs, he went with his mother. Everything Larry had wanted to avoid had happened. His fear of losing Haydon was almost unbearable.

Running, Falling, Just Keep Moving

Running Away

Larry Sr. was about ready to collapse. The emotion and fear he was feeling was as tight as a rubber band ready to break. He fell into bed unable to move, his blood pressure was sky high and he decided he had to leave. He asked Michelle if he could come spend a couple of days with her, as the pressure in our home was too much to take. He had to run, had to get away. With no sleep and the constant state of emotion in our home night after night, he was on overload. With tears running down my face barely able to breathe myself, I asked, I pleaded; "Please don't leave." I would be alone. How much was I supposed to take? He left.

I sat and cried, feeling abandoned, and feeling angry. "How could you do this to me? How could you walk out with all of this pain I feel?" I became numb inside as I decided what my action plan would be. When I am overwhelmed with emotion, the first thing I do is escape the emotion and turn to logic and that is what I did. "I will fix this. I will not just sit here and be a victim; I will not let this family fall apart." As if I had any control.

My first call was to dear friends John and Mary Jo from our Life Group. They lived near Michelle and Larry Sr. would respond to them.

In tears I called. "John I need your help. Can you and Mary Jo go to Michelle's and talk to Larry Sr.? He left and does not want to be here, too much pressure. He walked out, he just left. Could you please just talk to him?"

They went to Michelle's and spoke to Larry Sr. He was so broken and didn't know where to turn. They shared and prayed, but Larry Sr. stayed.

My next call was to a dear friend whose name is also Larry, "Larry, I need your help. Larry Sr. left and wants to stay at Michelle's for a few days. He just can't handle all the emotion, all the pressure. Can you go by and talk to him?"

He went to Michelle's and got there right after John and Mary Jo had left. He put Larry Sr. in his car and drove to the accident sight, sat, prayed, talked and cried. When they returned to Michelle's house Larry Sr. got in his car and came home, a bit more broken and withdrawn.

The darkness of our midnight hour comes, we cry, we scream and sometimes we run. We run because the pain of staying still and feeling is too difficult. Our minds think if we run fast enough the pain and hurt cannot catch us. We will outsmart our emotions, we will outsmart God. The confusion of the moment overtakes us and we cannot cope with life. Larry Sr. was there, in the darkness, in the confusion of the moment. The out of control emotion was too overwhelming for him. It was flight or die, run or ruin, which is what the person who has always thought they were in control does. That is what we all do at times, until you realize we are not the one who calls the shots. God is the one in control even in the most out of control situations. Oh, how this was an out of control situation.

God had his plan for each of us; He had a plan for our friends to help us and for Larry Sr. to see the love of that friend. God was in total control of this horrible situation. Did He like the circumstance? No. Did all that was happening surprise Him? No. You will never hear God say:

"I didn't know that," or "What a surprise that is."

God knew what Larry Sr. would do when the pressure cooker started to boil. He knew how much it would take to make Larry Sr. run and He knew who to put there for him, to reach out and as our friend put his arm around Larry Sr. God reached down and used our friend to touch him. Trust God completely, absolutely, however when you walk through the valley of the shadow of death, when you go into the waiting room or sit in your midnight hour you will still cry, scream, wail, and hurt deeply. You know in time, in God's time, the light will return one way or another. Yet the pain is still there, still real. It is like being on a stretching machine and you are being pulled apart from the inside out.

Falling Apart

What was wrong with all of this? Everyone is focusing on Larry Sr., this was not right. We were to be there for our son and help him, how we failed in so many ways. The focus went off of Larry and his brokenness and onto Larry Sr. and his fear and pain. This became a difficult time for Larry. He felt he had to take care of his dad and in no way would or could that be remotely possible. It put a wide crack in a relationship that was already cracked and would split in two over time. With each decision, each step through this crisis, another crack would form. Larry needed us to lean on completely and we were falling apart ourselves. In hindsight, we had not even gotten to the part where we could fall apart, we were still in survival mode and it was survival of the fittest. It seemed my job was to keep moving, keep planning this funeral. I felt if I stopped moving all the pieces that had broken inside me would literally fall to the ground and if that happened the pieces would disappear, I would disappear. If I kept moving the pieces would, in some miraculous way, stay put. The pieces just kept getting smaller and smaller and I could not move fast enough for inertia to keep them in place.

Michelle was desperately trying to hold her family together, be there for her brother in whatever way he needed her, support her mom and dad and in some small way keep the office going. Her family was falling apart, Tony with his escape of feelings could not escape the fact there was a funeral to go to. Each child was broken but none more than Hayley. Her young eight-year-old mind just could not understand. She was stoic during these first few days, not wanting to show any emotion just to be left alone. Dylan became quiet and withdrawn. Each night when we all met at our house, it was such a release, a reassurance for the children to see Haydon. Michelle would never be able to hold her family together like she wanted. So she chose to try and hold someone else together. She had to help someone. She had to get involved in something that took her mind off the problems, the emotions of the current crisis. Like me, she felt she had to keep moving, don't stop, keep doing, fixing, keep helping.

Changing the Focus

A few months prior to the accident Michelle had hired a young girl to work as a receptionist in our office. This young girl was a Christian and had shared with

Michelle and Larry her beliefs. However, there was something unusual about her, something that caused a red flag in my mind. The first time I knew there was definitely something wrong and my gut feelings were right, was at a dinner we had for the office staff. Usually the girls sat somewhat together and the guys would sit around each other to talk guy talk. This young girl wanted to sit next to one of our staff who was married and Larry stepped in and sat between them. The next few weeks I kept noticing that she was spending a lot of time in the company of this particular staff member and I asked Larry about this. He told me of his conversation telling them both that the flirting had to stop. It was inappropriate behavior for the office and for each of them as one was married and this young woman had just become engaged. The flirting stopped with the married staff and was replaced with Larry. When the staff was told of her engagement, she brought her wedding dress in for everyone to see. We sat at lunch and she casually mentioned a need to lose ten pounds before she got married. More red flags started waving.

After the accident, she came to our home on that Thursday evening and stayed the latest and sat with Larry and prayed with him. How great I thought that was, until it continued every night for weeks after the funeral. As it turned out, this young woman is bulimic and had some major personality and family problems. When we were trying to sleep she would stay in Haydon's bedroom and take cell phone calls into all hours of the morning from her boyfriend and mother. I was told her mother thought we were evil people trying to take control of her life. Her boyfriend was enraged with her actions, so Larry and Michelle decided they would help her. I guess they also thought, unconsciously, if they just kept moving and helping someone else their feelings of grief, the pieces of their soul, would not fall to the ground and get crushed. Larry, like the rest of us, felt the pain could not make him disappear if he just kept moving. With so much pain, we all focused on other things, other people, trying to run away emotionally.

All of this was going on at a time when we could not think ourselves out of a paper bag. I just needed to keep planning a funeral. Haydon was now with his mother; Monday night came in like mud sliding down the wall, dark and heavy. Just keep moving, don't stop or the mud will cover you up. Cry at night when you are alone, cry in the shower when you are alone, cry in the back yard when you are alone, and cry with your friends when Larry is not there. Just keep moving.

Support and Pain

The next few days all came and went as they ran together into one big moment. I had pictures we wanted to blow up and put up at the service and was told I had to get releases from the photographer, as they were copyright protected. So I had to contact the school for the phone number of the school photographer, contact Dolphin Quest in Hawaii, and have them each fax a release. All took time and helped to keep me from feeling the hurt and I got it all done. Both photographers were more than accommodating in giving their permission to use the photographs in anyway we wanted. I had to pick out some music for the video, and pictures, oh yes, go through all the pictures. Pick them out, put then in order, and get them to the church so the video could be made. Michelle had to get the obituary done and to the newspaper. Order flowers, order the doves to release at the service and decide what songs we want Elizabeth to sing. The list kept going on and so did the days. Our church offered to give friends or family their air miles if they needed to fly in for the service. People came every night. Larry had friends come over to support him. The house was full of beautiful flowers and plants. Hundreds of cards and letters came. Tears would flow as we read each one. How loved Heidi was, how loved we were, how much people wanted to reach out and touch us in some way. When you are hit by the ripples of a stone thrown into the water of your life, you get wet and sometimes the ripples knock you over. The community had been knocked over and everyone was reaching out to hold us up and help re-establish life's equilibrium.

One evening, some previous neighbors of Larry's came to visit. They walked in with a palm tree and a carved rock inscribed, "Heidi's Tree." What a beautiful gift. Friends brought books of which we all read with such hunger and urgency hunting for a way to miraculously avoid this grief. There must be a magic wand that we were missing. It had to be hidden in one of these books. So we read at night when we could not sleep. I would rise early in the morning and read and immediately break down in deep sobs. Mornings were my most difficult times. Heidi would get up early and come down stairs and sit with me and cuddle. She had gotten so she would bring her journal and write with me. She was just learning how to spell and she would make long lines to resemble written words. She would write stories that we now hold on to and cherish. How I miss her.

No one would be up at 5 A.M., so I could sit alone and cry. I knew Larry was up at night crying, I could hear him from our room. He tried to bury his sobs in the pillows but grief has a way of sneaking out under the closed door, even the closed door of our soul. I knew he was probably up early in his room crying alone. Why could we not share our grief, our tears with each other more? Why could we not hold each other, support each other in this terrible pain? We all wanted to be brave for the other one; we all thought that would help the other if they felt we were dealing with this horror. We all thought if we do not share these feelings maybe, just maybe, they will go away. We were all wrong.

Let Go and Let God

Thursday evening before the funeral our dear friends came in from Texas. They had told us they would be staying at a hotel but we insisted they stay with us, another one of my many *mistakes* in this journey into un-chartered waters. In my effort to keep everything *normal,* it never dawned on me that our life was not normal any more and no matter how hard I tried to change that, it would never change. My efforts only made things worse. I needed to let go and let God handle things and not override His ways. I felt if they spent the money to come all the way from Texas, we should at least let them stay with us. They wanted to be here to support us in this dreadful journey and grieve with us because they loved us and they loved Heidi.

They helped in getting the picture board ready to set in the foyer, helped Larry Sr. get his suit, carried in and out flowers and hugged us when we thought we could go no further. With all of their love around us, it was still an added stress. Deep inside I felt the responsibility to entertain and socialize. My heart did not want to do either. Just keep moving away from everyone and everything, nothing was more important than this service. All my strength had to be there for this day, and I had nothing left for sitting with my dear friends.

Again, Larry's grief and pain were put in the other room. He pulled back even more once our friends arrived. I could see his resentment and anger as he tried to understand our need and not his own. He could not share with these strangers. He could not share with us, he could not move beyond the pit he was in. How could I have turned my back on him that way? How alone he felt. No one could possibly understand the deep gaping hole that was growing inside and tearing apart every inch of his body. I wanted desperately to fix it for him but I too was being torn apart in the deep recess of my soul. I could not find a way out of this darkness. We all ran away from each other not knowing what to say or do. I prayed every night for a way to get through all of this, for the strength to walk through the day of the funeral, the rest of my life. My cry to God every night was, "Lord, show mercy on my family. Show me the way, clear my eyes, and give each of us the strength to prevail."

The Train of Survival

The Way We Were

As I look back, it was as if we each were given an evacuation notice to leave immediately or your life will be destroyed, no choice, no options. We all wanted to get to the same destination but each took a different road. We were all looking for the state of "The Way We Were" and wanted to live in towns called "Peace and Joy" and live on a street called "Happiness." At that time, little did we know, grief takes you out of the country through the desert of "Pain and Sorrow" and leaves you in the town of "Loneliness and Fear" living on the street named "Depression." Only when we reach the depths of the ghost town "Despair" and fall to our knees and cry out to God, will He start us on the road to the town of "Healing and Wholeness." No one in the family wanted this trip or even understood where it would take us, so we each grabbed our baggage and ran to catch the train called "Survival."

We all made the train but ended up in different cars. Larry got in the car called "Devastation and Fear" which would take him to the town of "Unforgiveness and Anger." Larry Sr. boarded the car called "Depression" that would take him to the town of "Unforgiveness and Fear." Both of these towns are next to each other and share the same mud hole. Michelle got on the train car called "Denial and Control" and there she scratched for control, any control that she could find. Any control would be better than none in her life. Tony boarded the train of "Control and Conquer." He thought if he could just regain control of his emotions and conquer and control his family, happiness would return. I boarded the train car of "Fight and Fix." This car took my focus off of the power of God in all situations and put it on my own ability to fix everything or should I say the lack of that ability. There was no way I was going to let my family fall apart, how wrong I was. The control was in God's hands not mine and He would prove that to me.

When we each started out, our eyes were on Larry, then the first stop came about the third day and each car was detached from the engine, from God's direction, and we all went on different roads. We became so burdened with the weight of our own baggage and blinded by our own grief and fears that we failed to see Larry and his pain; we never saw his need for us to carry him. I am not sure he would have allowed us to help him in that way, yet I do know it was our responsibility to put down our baggage and carry his and him if necessary. We all knew we had to get across the desert on the train of "Survival." So we each set out upon a lonely path carrying heavy bags and thirsting for relief. God allows us to make our own choices and pick our own roads. He knows what we will do and what it will take to get us *home*.

Clinched Hands

It took me about seven months to see and understand what we had done; at that time the light went on... each of us had our own journey. God could and would help us only when we release all of our feelings, all of our problems, into His hands. Each one of us was holding on to our fear and grief. We held on tightly, in clinched fists.

We had taken it out of God's hand and now, He needed to pull us back, because He loved us and had plans for each of our lives. I believe God wanted us to go on this journey hand in hand, soul to soul. However, I also believe God knew this is what we would do and He would use our choice to mold and shape each family member into the person He had planned us to be. We only had to allow Him to work and accept His way. In time of great distress and grief, we must come to Him with open hands in order to let go of the pain and accept His blessings. As long as our hands are clinched we cannot release the fear and in the dark moist clutches of our fist, the seed of fear sprouts and grows into our very veins and becomes the anger, resentment and un-forgiveness that pull us down into the quicksand of sin.

How deep the hurt to know there was nothing I could do to help Larry. The time for that had passed and his journey would be longer and harder than any of ours, for he carried an extra heavy piece of baggage, the loss of his future with his daughter and the fear for the safety of his son. Turning this over to God was and is difficult for him, yet it will be the only way to quench the thirst as he walks through the desert. How I want to be able to give him the cup he needs to quench his thirst and take the burden away. By stepping in, I would be getting in between him and God. If I have learned anything it has been let God do it. Only in this way will God receive the glory and that is what it is all about.

Released

Saturday, May 9, 2003 was the day we buried Heidi Nicole Nix. Born March 9, 1995, went *home* to be with Jesus April 29, 2003. The shock continued. This could not be real. The physical pain was almost unbearable . . . almost. God showed mercy on me, on my family.

Family and close friends along with our staff were at the graveside service at 10 A.M. We got up early to get ready for this day that no one should ever have to get ready for. The distractions continued with the arrival of the young woman from the office. Haydon was with his Dad and would be riding with him to the service. Larry dressed and got Haydon dressed in their new suits, how handsome they looked. Heidi would have been so proud of her brother and Daddy. Our friends rode with Larry Sr. and I decided to ride with Larry, Haydon and friend. Larry reached out to this young woman as a distraction in order to get through the day, however, grief has a way of flowing over distraction into your soul and you melt at its touch.

The graveside was beautiful. The pastor from Heather's church gave the eulogy first. He did not know Heidi and I was somewhat glad for it seemed impersonal to me and made what was a day in the fog easier. As he finished, Dave stepped in and gave us wonderful words of love and support. He ended by requesting we each give one another a "Heidi hug." We had white doves for each person who wanted to release one in memory of Heidi. Each person had his or her own reason for wanting to do this. It was usually a symbol of releasing your loved one. It was a beautiful symbol, yet in my heart it was impossible to release Heidi. The symbol has been replayed in my mind a thousand times. Heidi was held by no person and therefore, could not be released.

We are to hold our loved ones in an open hand for if we hold them in a tight fist they cannot grow, they cannot soar like the eagles, and God cannot use them. Our children are blessings given to us by God, on loan, to love, to rear, and then to let go. Everything in life is on loan to us and can be taken back in an instant. God gives and He can take away, as He is the creator of us all and everything here on earth. God loves us so much He will do anything to save us, to reach us, to bring us *home.* If I keep my hand open, then when it is time for my blessings to leave, I do not have to release them for they are God's and free to go at anytime and I count myself richly blessed to have been on the top of the mountain.

    My time with Heidi was such a blessing, a time to be on top of the mountain. God gave her to the world for a short few years. In those years Heidi taught me much about love and forgiveness and then Jesus called her *home.* We never possessed Heidi, so it was to me, impossible to release her. What I let go that day was my future with a beautiful granddaughter. In retrospect, I let go of my entire family. God had wanted me to let them go, to get out of His way, so He could help them become what He wanted and fulfill His plans in their life. God's plan would be fulfilled in spite of me. Larry was to make a harsh break from our family and Michelle's family would be torn apart. My own relationship with my husband was to become more strained than ever. The loss, the grief continued on and on and on. My life as I knew it flew away that day as I began to understand what letting go truly means.

Heidi and Her Hugs

Touched by an Angel

Let me introduce you to Heidi. From the day she was born March 9, 1995, her connection to her Daddy was strong. As with most first children, mom and dad were nervous and anxious about their abilities to parent. Heidi's mom wanted to nurse so very badly and she felt a bit of pressure from her family, as they truly believed she should nurse. However, being the high strung young woman she was, that was not to be. So from the beginning, there was tension between mom and Heidi and Heidi cried, a lot.

They lived in an area on the outskirts of Orange County and had to drive in traffic every day to and from work. Heidi would cry the entire way into town and then home again. Each day they would come by, and Larry Sr. and I would have the opportunity of holding Heidi and walking or rocking with her. Larry Sr. has always had a way with babies. He could walk for hours with a crying child; he was so calm with her. Eventually, they found her stomach was distended from over feeding. Even when her diet settled down, the crying did not stop. I used to watch Heather and Larry with Heidi and marvel at their patience as they would put her in the car seat and she would be screaming and stiffening her legs in resistance. I believed at the time they were angels with her. I look back and have no doubt it was the other way around. Heidi was reflecting the strain between the two of them. As the tension was growing between them in their relationship Heidi was screaming to them, "Let it go, work it out, for me, for me."

Heidi loved to laugh and roughhouse with her Daddy or grandpa. From the time she started getting around on her own, from crawling to staggering steps Heidi was headed in her own direction. She loved her bath and water, from playing with the hose or swimming in a pool. Heidi excelled in anything requiring balance. Heidi shared her Daddy's love of camping and riding in the jeep. Larry enjoyed taking Heidi on new experiences and watching her excitement of seeing an animal for the first time or watching a bug crawl across the ground. Her animated looks and responses were wonderful and he lived for each one.

Everyone who knew Heidi always talked about her hugs. No one had a hug like Heidi. You knew you had been hugged when Heidi hugged you. Her hugs were big, warm, tight, and reassuring as Heidi gave her entire self to you through a hug. You had not really ever experienced a hug until you had a "Heidi Hug."

Heidi was faced with grown up issues at a very young age in her life. Haydon was born when Heidi was two and before he celebrated his first birthday, Larry and Heather's marriage ended. Heidi was three and could not understand why Daddy did not come home any more. Larry moved in with us and I count every second he lived with us as a blessing. Heidi and Haydon became our children, grand.

Heidi would call at night and cry wanting Daddy to come home but it was not to be. We made a special room for each one of them. We had moved into a five-bedroom home the December before, of which I believe God designed, so each one of the grandchildren could have their own room. God had His plan for us and the blessing of having Larry, Heidi and Haydon with us for five years was in His plan. No one can understand how blessed I was to have had this time with Heidi. God showered me with His amazing grace and the blessing of Heidi's life.

Heidi took care of her brother from day one. She decided Daddy needed her to help with Haydon each time they were with us. From making sure they had diapers to helping feed Haydon, Heidi was there. Haydon grew to depend on Heidi as much if not more than his mom and dad. She would speak and translate for Haydon as he struggled with his speech.

Heidi learned to swim in the backyard pool and excelled. Her sleek body screamed athlete. When she was four we took a trip to Arizona with the entire family. Standing in the elevator we were asked if she was a gymnast. Many times over her short life people would ask about her athletic ability. She was thin with well-defined arm and leg muscles. From birth her hair was blond and un-controllably curly. Not until she was seven did her hair grow out enough to pull the curls down. She loved to have it straightened, yet I loved to see it curly. Her big blue eyes would peek out from the morning curls with such brightness and excitement.

Heidi never met a stranger. She was very direct, as she got older. Hayley and Heidi became close friends, as they were only five months apart, an attachment that was beyond understanding to many. From the time they were babies the two girls bonded. From what they wore to secret giggles, they were so very close. What each one lacked in ability the other one made up for. Both would tell us how everyone thought they were twins. Hayley being the taller of the two, with dark eyes and straight dark hair, they were far from twins. Hayley loved Heidi's athletic ability and Heidi loved Hayley's intelligence. Heidi always encouraged Hayley in learning something athletic and Hayley was an example to Heidi of effort put into learning. How they helped each other.

Both would stay after school and go from room to room inquiring if they could be of help to any teacher. Heidi had started helping a little boy in school who had a learning disability. This little boy was a difficult child and he was not responding to any of the teachers. Heidi stepped in and would instruct him with her directness and love. She would point her finger at him and tell him, "Now you listen to Heidi." As he started responding to Heidi's direction he looked forward to his time with her. The school was planning on moving this special little boy into the same class with Heidi the following year so she could continue this special relationship. What would he do now, who would help this little boy, who would God use in place of Heidi?

If you wanted something Heidi had, she would give it to you. Whether it was something she was eating or something she was playing with, it was yours. She knew it would be replaced with something better, something beyond comprehension. She gave of herself without fear, to the end. I enjoyed the weekends and days Heidi was with us. We would usually have a party, which meant friends would come over or we would just barbeque outside. Heidi was there to help cook, set the table and serve. How she loved to be the "waitress," take orders and then get a tip. Heidi and I would usually go shopping once a month. When it was possible we took Hayley so they could get matching outfits. They had very different tastes and as they got older, the matching outfits started to slow down. As their bodies were changing shape, each one chose the clothes that best suited them.

They both embraced these differences and continued to encourage each other. Heidi was the first to tell Hayley if something looked good on her and Hayley would support Heidi in whatever she chose. They truly understood unconditional love.

We had a special shopping spree before our trip to Hawaii. Finding bathing suits for the two girls proved to be a challenge. Each was allowed four bathing suits and if we could not find the perfect one before we left we would buy them in Hawaii. Hayley found all four of her suits on our shopping spree and Heidi found only three. While in Hawaii, we bought Heidi a leopard print, one-piece bathing suit. The one piece was the unusual part; the leopard print was her style. The day after we arrived home she had to model the suit for her Daddy. It was the last time she was in the swimming pool; the last time we shared her infectious laugh. Heidi had an understanding of Hayley's insecurity and fragileness and she would tell me how we needed to help Hayley. Her heart was tender toward everyone. Yet having a tender heart also made her vulnerable to the hurts from others.

When Heidi would do homework or try to accomplish a new task, she wanted desperately to please her Daddy, above all others. She had been struggling in her reading and math and would have meltdowns while doing homework. Heidi's last few months in school were exciting for her as she had finally *got it* and was starting to excel. She was so excited to be taking the SAT 9 testing that was to begin the day she died.

When Heidi had an emotional meltdown, she would cry big crocodile tears and her face would turn blotchy red. It would take her awhile to calm herself down and return to a relaxed state. I remember one evening in particular. Her dad was working in the garage on his jeep and Heidi and I were preparing dinner. Hayley was spending the night as the three of us were going to run in the Los Angeles Race for the Cure the next morning. We had gone out and bought matching shirts and running shorts. I had to take Heidi's shorts in, as her legs were not big enough to fill in the shorts. We had fixed spaghetti and the table was set for everyone. We all came in for dinner and Heidi spilled a glass of orange drink, accidents happen. Larry got very upset with Heidi and started yelling at her about not paying attention. Larry Sr. stepped in wanting to protect Heidi from getting in trouble, telling Larry it was an accident; they got into a big argument. Heidi ended up having a major melt-down feeling she had disappointed her Daddy. Larry told her she could not go to the race the next day and she was devastated. Between feeling responsible for spilling a drink and then feeling responsible for the argument between her dad and grandpa and then not being able to go to the race she was extremely upset. Hayley sat quietly hoping no one would notice her as she ate and ate until everyone had left. I was crying and upset. I cleaned up the spill and held Heidi once Larry went back outside. She cried and I reassured her it would be ok and she would be able to go and I would finish fixing her shorts. She had wanted so very badly to please her Daddy with a nice dinner, yet one accident and her life for the night was ruined. I really do not think Larry even knew how deeply she was hurt that night because Heidi would forgive and love her Daddy in an instant, even more.

So many times we all, as parents, make the same mistake, tired and distracted our focus is on our need. Our children have an accident, drop something, spill something and we blow. We make something big out of something so trivial. Larry allowed Heidi to go to the race the next day and we had a wonderful time. She ran her heart out. No one could have known in a few short months Heidi would not have to worry about pleasing anyone anymore.

"Do you not know that in a race all the runners run, but only one gets the prize? Run in such a way as to get the prize." I Corinthians 9:25 (NIV)

    Heidi has received the prize.
    Heidi had a dream catcher hanging over her bed that her Daddy had bought her the February before her death. She kept her parents wedding picture under her pillow the last few months of her life. Every night she would say her prayers. Every night she would read with her Daddy or come down and sit with me and we would read a bible story. She had started waking up early on the weekends to watch the sun come up and loved to sit outside with Poppy (grandpa) and watch the sun set. Her trips camping in the camper were her favorite times with her Daddy and Haydon. She helped pick out the purple sheets and blankets for the camper. Outside was her favorite place to be. Running, playing, swimming, riding her bike, playing soccer, playing tetherball and just being with other kids, anything outside, with others, was where Heidi wanted to be.
    Heidi was a special young girl. In many ways as I look back, she was truly our angel. She taught us so much about love and giving and forgiveness. How she modeled Jesus in her tenderness and how she touched our lives. Heidi had a tender heart for others and put others first. She always thought of her brother and Hayley and gave words of encouragement and love. She forgave and

continued on in her walk. Heidi had a wonderful sense of humor and would kid you and set you up for a joke. Her laugh was infectious. She loved music, dance and art, so many memories of her putting on a show for us. Usually with Hayley, the two would sing and dance. She had started drawing pictures for everyone. Give her a pen or pencil and paper and soon you would have a picture of her family or what she had done the day before. I hold dear to my heart a picture she drew of me with hearts around it. I hold so tightly to the little things I have left of her. When packing up her room, I cleaned out her hair brush and put the hair in an envelope, something, anything, I could touch, to remember. Remembering is bitter sweet. The wonderful times we laughed and cuddled, cried and hugged, played and prayed together. She was in many ways wise beyond her years. God truly blessed us with this angel.

One Big Happy Family

A Blessing from God

Just a short time before Heidi's death, we had all of our children and grandchildren living with us. Michelle and Tony had a flood in their home and could not live there for a year and eight months while the remodeling was taking place. We had eleven people living in our home, six grandchildren ranging in ages from 0 to 9 and five very different, very independent adults. Everything was always in a pile, always busy, always something going on. The children rode to school together, cooked together, bathed together, shopped together, went to church together and slept together. We were one big *happy* family. What a blessing God gave our entire family. I must say at the time, I was not sure this was a blessing yet with all of the events in our life that followed God's hand was definitely on us.

There were many nights my husband and I would sit in our room wondering how in the world we would get through this. Today, I sit and recall how wonderful every moment was. How that experience ultimately gave hope to four small children whose father left them. They had seen Heidi and Haydon not only survive but blossom with their dad through a difficult divorce. All of the children grew close to each other and their aunts and uncles. They also learned being different was ok. Each person was very different in their personalities and in their abilities, yet they all grew to accept and understand those differences and felt loved by the entire family. How blessed I was and am for having had this experience. God is amazing and so good.

Larry's Pain

How does grief work in the mind? Its tentacles stretch out and hit every fiber of your being. Like internal invaders that take over every part of your heart, your body and your mind. The tentacles reach far and deep and leave nothing untouched by its penetrating ugliness. Larry would walk a path in his life few would or could walk. He was born January 23, 1968 a big beautiful baby of 10 lbs., our second child of two. He loved to be held and rocked. I hold on to the memories of holding him and singing to him. He loved to sit next to me and cuddle and be read to and held. He was an easy baby until he was around ten months old.

He began having ear infections and it was a trip to the doctor every month for yet another prescription. This continued until he was two years old. His behavior had become difficult as you would tell him not to do something and he would look at you and then continue doing the one thing you told him not to. At two years old, the doctors decided to take his tonsils out. That was a very hard time for both Larry and me. I wanted to stay with him in the hospital, he was so frightened, but the doctors would not let me. I don't know who cried more. I do know he was so afraid to stay there; I stayed until he fell asleep and then came back early the next morning to pick him up and reassure him I would not leave. Once the surgery was complete, they found out Larry had been deaf for several months and possibly over a year, which explained why his speech was behind in development. It also explained why his behavior had deteriorated. The guilt was agonizing. What had we done to this little boy, how could we ever make it right? We never could, for as much as we tried it would never be. The damage was done. We went to counselors and I read books and nothing we did seem to be right.

When Larry was eight years old, he was diagnosed as an ADD child. Not hyperactive, just attention deficient. He was later diagnosed with long-term memory loss. What had I done wrong? As Larry grew up his speech straightened out with speech therapy. At one time, his voice was raspy and we took him to a specialist and they found he was straining his voice. He tried not to speak so loudly so his larynx would not be destroyed but even today he has a loud voice. Every year I would meet with his teachers, coaches and principles to discuss his ADD. Most were not trained in this area. At that time, there were no books, no special classes or training to be had for ADD children. Most were put on Ritalin, that way the parents and teachers would not have to worry about the needs of these children, they just walked around numb, but no trouble to the schools or at home. We did not choose to go this route. We continued on with teacher meetings, and counseling.

A year and a half after Heidi's death, I picked up a book I had bought several months prior and started to read about ADD children and adults. Oh, the regrets, the insight, and the pain of what I had done to my child. Why did I not read it sooner? I had been lead by God to buy the book and I laid it down to read later. Oh God, am I too late?

His pain was fathoms deeper than I could have ever thought. Not just the pain of Heidi, but the pain that he had gone through his whole life from teachers, coaches, his parents, his ex-wife. All ignorant, all abusive in his terms, all so caught up in their own needs never wanting to stop, be real and see this little boy, this man, for who he is. If you have a child, a spouse, a co-worker that you think is ADD, read about it and learn about it. There is nothing wrong with these children, or adults. Their brains are wired different from ours, not worse or better just different. They are loving children and adults, more in touch with their feelings than most. They are creative and intuitive. They read people very well, usually do not like to be touched and have emotional out-bursts of anger, which result from the emotional pain they feel. They use this anger to build a wall between you and them in order to protect themselves from any further pain. If you love them, find out about them. Their love is deep, as deep as their pain.

Where Do We Go From Here

The Funeral Ends

Heidi's memorial service was everything Larry wanted it to be. He had conceded to allow his father to speak on behalf of our family. I was glad he did as three family members from his ex-wife's family spoke, including Heather. The video was beautiful with the pictures of Heidi at all ages ending with a touching "I'll miss you, Love Hayley." Hayley sat in the pew and sobbed uncontrollably, there would be no stoic escape from this emotional service. The music was touching and Dave's eulogy was heartfelt. Seven hundred people sat and cried as we remembered Heidi. I was overcome with so many different feelings of love and sadness all at the same time. Love from family and friends, and sadness to think of what could have been in Heidi's life. Many people came because she was only eight-years old and they sat clutching their own fears and some clutching their own child. The firemen and paramedics came to see what this little girl really looked like. They wanted to erase the horrific pictures in their minds and replace them with pictures of a beautiful little girl whom they never knew. People came who had read about her death in the newspapers. Teachers and school friends came in hope of some closure, some relief to this painful time. People came because the ripples from the stone had hit them hard and we sat, wet with tears. Whatever the reason, they came and we were touched.

Our Life Group from church had arranged to have all the food handled after the service. They had sandwiches, salads, cookies and drinks for everyone. They had arranged for Kleenex in the pews, people working in the parking lot. Even our senior minister was helping set up the flowers on the podium. Friends volunteered to hand out programs and stand at the memory books. After the service, several members of the church along with some from our Life Group took all of the flowers to the graveside. Every detail was handled, covered by our Life Group and our church family. How blessed we were and continue to be with the outpouring of love that surrounded us.

The day before the service we had taken picture boards of Heidi to be placed at the entrance of the sanctuary to allow people to see as much of Heidi as possible. How my heart was breaking, this was our last chance to touch the world, to impact others for Heidi. I wanted so very much to stand on the rooftop and shout out how special she was and have my words echo to the end of time, words that would turn to pictures and come to life for everyone to know who Heidi was and is in heaven. But that would and could not happen. We had this one-day and then back to what was now a different reality.

On Automatic

The day came and went, and as I collapsed on my bed that night it was hard to turn my mind off. I kept going back over every detail of the day, every word, every song, every picture. I wanted to remember every detail, in this way I would not lose my memories; I could hold on just a little bit longer, she would not be gone.

The next day was Mother's Day and I got up to

go to church. I remember people being surprised that Michelle, Larry Sr. and I were there. We were still in survival mode, we were the robots and going to church on Sundays is what we did. Everything was on automatic, our brain was not reasoning at all. As we sat in the back of the church with our friends sitting between Michelle and us, I was numb. Why was I not sitting next to my daughter, holding her, crying with her? I cried uncontrollably. After church, our friends took us to lunch down by the beach. Again, I was numb. When we got home all I wanted to do was to run and hide. Emotionally exhausted I went upstairs to my room and went to bed. Our dear friends left to visit some of their relatives as they were leaving the next day. Depression was taking over, nothing more to do, just cry, stay numb and cry.

Back to Work

Monday came too quickly and I was not prepared to enter into the business world. Larry needed to take some time off and I needed to support him in that. Back to work with a mind that could hardly process routine daily activities. So I jumped in with both feet even though I felt like I was drowning. Nothing, I repeat nothing, was normal; everything was difficult.

> *"Trust in the Lord with all your heart and lean not on your own understanding; in all your ways acknowledge him, and he will make your paths straight." Proverbs 3:5–6 (NIV)*

I got through each day surprising myself, still feeling numb and trusting God with each step. I knew we had to get into counseling, I could feel the family disappearing. At the urging of the Holy Spirit I called a counselor.

I contacted a counseling group that had been referred to me by our pastor. I called and got an appointment for the family. Larry, Michelle, Tony, Larry Sr. and myself, all with one counselor to help the family grieve together and understand how the grief was affecting each of us individually. When we first met with the counselor, I told her I did not want my family to fall apart. Little did I understand my desires were not God's desires and our family would walk a road each chose, heart broken and torn to pieces.

Focusing on Someone Else's Problem

A few days before the funeral, the young women from our office had told Larry and Michelle she was quitting her job and entering a rehab program. Michelle decided to help her with Larry's blessing. Michelle talked her into staying until her insurance took effect, which was only a couple of weeks away. Larry decided to help her get her own car so she could break away from a controlling family and boyfriend, get into rehab and take control of her own life. Hindsight tells me they both wanted to help someone else since they could not help their selves or Heidi. Their emotions were all over the map and they both believed they could focus on someone else's problems and not have to face their own. Again, hindsight being 20/20, if you cannot handle your own emotions and feelings, stay out of someone else's problems. Larry helped her get a car and Michelle got her into a rehab program, which the insurance would pay. No problem, wrong, big problem.

The rehab for this young girl was to run for a few weeks and at the end of this time she would need a stable, supportive place to stay. Michelle decided she could stay with her family. Michelle and her family had no place asking a sick young women struggling with bulimia to come into their home and live. Hayley was so vulnerable at this time and they were setting her up for another hurt. Larry talked to Michelle about her decision and they agreed it would not be the best decision to have her move in and stay there, until -

Split in Half

Feeling Betrayed

July 4th is a day we have friends and family over to eat, swim and enjoy the fireworks. This year was to be a big party as Larry was scheduled to have both of his children and Heidi loved helping with the parties, but this year Heidi would not be with us. Larry had felt it would be a good day to have friends and family over to share this lonely day with. I planned, invited and cooked to the point of exhaustion. It was a stifling hot day and not much of a breeze. Friends and family came to show their support and love for us. It was a day of tears and laughter remembering our ray of sunshine. The one odd thing that stood out in my mind was Michelle and Tony's behavior. When they walked in the door I knew something was wrong. They were quiet, withdrawn, and angry. Not being ones to show their anger it showed up in resentfulness of having to be there. It was something I felt when they walked in the door, like darkness had just walked in; the air seemed to become hotter and heavier.

"Why did you have this party? It is too soon after Heidi's death to be celebrating."

"Larry did nothing to help; you should have cancelled the party."

"This is inappropriate. I do not want to be here, we are leaving early."

The truth was Michelle was going to see the young women in question and she had decided to betray her brother. Betrayal is harsh, hurtful and guilt producing. Webster's Dictionary describes betrayal as "To fail or desert in a moment of need." Larry had a need to be supported in his confused state, a need to be carried in his brokenness. Michelle also had a need, to get in control of her life in any way she could find, even if it meant betraying her brother. To choose any other direction would have created a mental depression that she could not handle at that time. Grief and loss work their darkness into every area of our lives; it can split you mentally in half.

Michelle and Tony talked about this young women and Tony suggested to Michelle that if her desire was to help this young girl, by letting her move in, then she should go ahead with it no matter what Larry or her parents thought. Again I will go back to hindsight. Remember, Tony had boarded the train of "Control and Conquer." To accomplish control he had to get rid of any influences over Michelle, which meant he must also divide. He could not conquer her and control if anyone else had input and here was the perfect splitting point. And split it did.

Mount Saint Helens

In our next family counseling session Larry blew. In a typical ADD fashion the anger came out like the eruption of Mt. St. Helens. In abusive language he expressed his feelings in no uncertain terms. The split between Larry and Michelle reached its all time low. It split Larry Sr. and me against Michelle and Tony, yet out of fear we concealed our thoughts as we sank lower and lower. Again, not supporting Larry, we road the fence fearful of loosing our family. With blinders on we could not see we had already lost. If ever put in a position to choose sides with children, choose the one that is morally right. God will support you and guide you through this most difficult time.

To this day, I believe the counselor could have interceded in the situation but was not sure which way to go. I believe she felt the tension but read it as something different. I am not sure she had ever dealt with such deep passion and strong emotion before. All through the session Larry wanted to talk, he kept trying to address his passion, but she never allowed him to speak until finally he took his stand at the end of the session. By then he was beyond control, he had little time to say what should have been shared from the beginning in a controlled manner. It was like trying to suppress a volcano, you can walk around it and fly over it but when it is ready to blow there is nothing you can do but stand back, and get out of the way of the hot, penetrating lava. So it was with Larry's hurt turned to anger. He felt betrayed by his sister. She chose a stranger over family. She chose to support a stranger and not see Larry's brokenness and fear. She chose it because it was easier to help someone you are not emotionally attached to, than to reach out and share in the devastation of someone you love. She chose it because Tony supported her in this decision and it felt like she had some control in her life. She chose it because it was too difficult to face her own loss, her own fears. Heidi had been gone for less than three months and already grief and fear was tearing at the thin thread that held our family together. Were these threads so fragile they could not withstand the assault of Satan? How would this end, how much more could this family take? Little did I know we would continue to be assaulted as God was permitting our family to be tested.

"God I am on my knees, I have given you my family, my life, show me Your way, give me wisdom, hold me up, and restore my family." I pleaded daily.

> *"This is the confidence we have in approaching God: that if we ask anything according to his will,* (according to his will, his time not mine) *he hears us. And if we know that he hears us–whatever we ask–we know that we have what we asked of him." I John 5:14–15 (NIV)*

Running From God

The blackness of grief had covered our family. Its cold knife had cut deep into the very soul of each person. The confusion of where to place our anger, our fear, was causing us to run any direction but to God. We were out of control. We could not be mad at God, could we? We could not be mad at Heather, or were we? We could not be mad at the policemen or firemen; after all they did their job, or did they? We could not be mad at each other, what did each of us have to do with Heidi's death, but we were. Misplaced anger grew out of control. The serpent raised its ugly head and attacked our family, our closely-knit, dysfunctional, boundary-less family and each of us stood, frozen in fear not knowing what to do. I prayed every day for mercy, healing and understanding, for love and peace to return to our family. God was moving at His pace not mine, God was working in each life according to His plan.

> *"Praise be to the Lord, for he has heard my cry for mercy. The lord is my strength and my shield; my heart trusts in him, and I am helped." Psalm 28:6–7 (NIV)*

Each of us went into counseling separately. Larry never returned to counseling with the family. He desperately needed to begin his healing and he now knew it would be a journey to be taken alone. He began building a fence to protect his property, to protect his heart and soul. Only he could do this and it was going to take some drastic steps. He went to his counselor that had helped him through his divorce. Larry Sr. and I selected a counselor to help us, not only through our grief, but also to heal the brokenness of the past and attempt to rebuild a hurting relationship. Michelle chose a counselor to help her through the grief and brokenness she was feeling about herself and her relationship in her marriage. Tony remained in our group counseling, of which would be short lived. Haydon along with Hayley and Dylan were each seeing their own counselors. All of us grieving, hurting, bleeding from this devastation and not knowing how to keep from bleeding to death.

Torn Apart by Bitterness

Our family never denied the grief and difficulty we were having in getting through and dealing with the loss of Heidi. We just did not know how this grief would rip us apart and bring to the surface all of the problems we did not want to talk about or the problems we did deny.

With grief you are attempting to push down on the pain, so much so, that you start pushing out all the other emotions and they come spewing out like pus; the lies, the family secrets, they all come spurting out with no control. In many areas of our life we had buried our feelings; we had buried the living dead. The problem with that is the living dead will rise again with added strength. We talked to each other about what our perceptions were and we sought help both in prayer and counseling. We each knew this journey would not be quick or easy we just did not know how long and hard it would be.

What was once viewed, as a *close family* from the outside was now a family torn apart by bitterness and anger. Over the next few months, friends would reach out to each of us not knowing what to say or do as we each kept slipping deeper into despair. Michelle's marriage would end shortly before the one-year anniversary of Heidi's death. Her husband wanted to go away and *be happy*. His inability to identify and process deep feelings put him on a road of fear, and that fear drove him further away from his family. He would tell you it was all Michelle's fault, however, his background of hurt and abandonment was to raise its head and call out to be repeated. I have found that we all want to repeat the brokenness in our background because it is what we know and change creates too much fear. We are always comfortable with what we know even if it is craziness. We cannot stand to change our lives no matter how hurtful and hard the current situation is. To change the programming done by our family of origin creates mental chaos. It becomes easier to run and re-create the sickness than to expend effort and change. If we are to grow in our lives we must change. Change is inevitable, growth is not, growth is a choice.

Our Children's Children

Not only did four beautiful children lose a precious friend and cousin, they now had the rejection and abandonment of their father to deal with. I truly believe only God can protect a child and bring them through such difficult times in life. There will come a time when each of these children will choose their own paths. They must choose either a path towards Jesus or the path to repeat their father's sins.

> *"The Lord, the compassionate and gracious God, slow to anger, abounding in love and faithfulness, maintaining love to thousands, and forgiving wickedness, rebellion and sin. Yet he does not leave the guilty unpunished; he punishes the children and their children for the sin of the fathers to the third and fourth generation." Exodus 34: 6b-7 (NIV)*

How this scripture resonates in my mind. I do not want my children to be punished for my sin or for past generations sin. I pray daily to break the bond of past generations and to live a life of faithfulness for my children and their children. We all need to look at ourselves and our relationship with God. When we walk through the darkness we are to change and grow in our wisdom of God's word. Ask what we are to learn from these experiences, from these challenges, for our actions will affect the future of our grandchildren.

We are warned not to impede the trust children have in God. We are told of the price we pay for turning our children away.

> *"And whoever welcomes a little child like this in my name welcomes me. But if anyone causes one of these little ones who believe in me to sin, it would be better for him to have a large millstone hung around his neck and to be drowned in the depths of the sea." Matthew 18:5–6 (NIV)*

Yet we all continue on a path destined to bring us into the depths of the sea. How strong our flesh is, how strong the call to turn away, how strong the program in our minds from childhood, change has to start some place. "Dear Lord, let change start with me."

By accepting the compassion and graciousness of God, by accepting His abounding love and faithfulness, I turn away from the sins of my parents in order to make a difference in my children and grandchildren, so God will bless them as an inheritance from their parents.

> *"See, I set before you today life and prosperity, death and destruction. For I command you today to love the Lord your God, to walk in his ways, and to keep his commands, decrees and laws; then you will live and increase, and the Lord your God will bless you . . ."*
> *Deuteronomy 30:15–16 (NIV)*

This is a daily walk, a daily choice, a daily struggle to accept God's grace which gives me strength to continue on my journey.

The Truth and Nothing but the Truth So Help Me God

Finding the Truth

Larry continued being pulled from every angle. He was not able to handle the depth of his pain so he turned to finding, searching, for the truth of the accident. He wanted to know the truth; he wanted someone to be responsible for his daughter's death. He set out on a journey to find what actually happened to his precious Heidi.

It took several months to receive a police report. The police continued telling him; "Let the process work." He met several times with the police and with the district attorney. All were touched by his loss, showed compassion and assured him they were doing everything possible to complete a thorough investigation.

When Larry finally received the police report he noticed there were many loose ends that did not make sense. The report stated that everyone at the scene had been interviewed. The accident was not caused due to speeding, Heather was not on the cell phone, and the truck was not doing anything wrong, taillights worked, it was just an accident. She ran into the back of a stopped truck by accident? How can that happen? The report for both the fire department and police departments were not filled out by the first officer on scene nor was procedure followed in which everyone at the scene was to submit a report. The reports were based on second and third hand information from each person there. The interviews of witnesses were botched and incomplete. Nothing made sense, nothing in the reports showed how the accident happened. How do you run into the back of a stopped truck? Larry contacted a family friend that was an attorney and he put Larry in touch with an investigator who would look into the accident and help discover the truth. He had to know, we all wanted to know.

The Picture is Blurry

When you lose a child to such a tragedy and you cannot deal with this amputation, you continue on day after day in survival mode. You must focus on something other than your pain. Larry began focusing on the cause of the accident. This is not an uncommon process, you want answers and you go to extreme measures to get them. Accountability is big when there has been an accident and someone dies, especially a child. Being struck by lightening is an act of God. Slipping on a wet bathroom floor and hitting your head on the bathtub is an accident. Running into the back of a truck, which results in a death, is not an accident. Something was wrong, the picture was blurry.

God works in wonderful ways even when you are trying to do everything yourself and not in His way. My sister-in-law's son was getting married. The mother of the young women he was to marry worked as the city clerk in the town of the accident. We were printing their wedding invitations and she happened to mention that an award was being given to a retired fireman that was first on scene of the car accident that killed Heidi. The award was for his help in maintaining calm at this devastating accident. My husband and I decided to attend this meeting to thank him for his help. I gave the information to our son, thinking he may want to attend this event, he did not. But as Larry looked over the interview list searching for this person's name, he found it was never mentioned.

He lived on one of the street corners where the accident had occurred. He heard the crash and came out, immediately went to the car and attempted to calm Heather while they waited for the paramedics. This first person on the scene was never interviewed, this was big or so we thought. In a later interview the ex-fireman stated with the extent of the tragedy and damage to Heidi, he kept his focus on the mother, he could not say where Heidi was sitting or anything about the accident. This lack of detail in the police report spurred Larry to continue on. He knew in his heart something was wrong.

The Pain of Reality

Larry's hobby is re-building jeeps and because of this, he is familiar with the salvage yards and the process of selling and dismantling a totaled car. He decided he wanted to see if he could purchase the car Heidi had been killed in. This may have been a way to stay close to Heidi, to touch the last thing she touched, I don't really know. There was also a need, in his eyes, to keep the car in case the DA wanted to pursue and prosecute the case of which Larry wanted desperately to happen. He had been told the police department had released the car, which was confusing since the investigation was supposedly ongoing.

After contacting the insurance company, they

informed Larry, the police had released the car and "It has been put in line to be auctioned off." He called the local salvage yard where the insurance company told him the car was stored. It was not there. He contacted the insurance company again and the response this time, they had *lost* the folder and could not locate the car. All the delay tactics and attempts to subdue his interest in the car only fueled his persistence. Because of his knowledge in this industry he knew where to go next. He contacted a salvage yard almost 50 miles away and found the car. It had conveniently been picked up and taken 50 miles out of town. The average person would have never found the car; it would have been sold and dismantled without ever being looked at. Before he was able to see the car, he had to have permission from the insurance company. This took some time, as the insurance company was not eager to have Larry see the car. After conversations between the DA, the police, investigators and insurance company, the insurance company reluctantly agreed.

A date was set for Larry to meet his investigator at the salvage site. The investigator came with multiple rolls of film, his jump suit to put on over his cloths for crawling around and under the car and an eye for detail. The site of the car created a multitude of emotions in Larry. The damage to the car was beyond belief. The impact was so violent that it had literally ripped the top of the Toyota 4Runner off. It was obvious there was little, if any, breaking done before impact. He realized how blessed he was that Haydon had survived. He also realized there was much more to the accident than the police or fire department had reported. The investigator was able to establish the angle of impact and approximate speed along with facts such as when and how breaking had occurred. The biggest and most difficult piece of information that came from this heart wrenching investigation was the cold hard fact; Heidi did not have her seat belt on.

Both reports had said she was sitting behind her mother, buckled in. Both reports were wrong. No one even bothered to find out what had happened. No one took the time to find out the real reason this little girl was killed. No one took the time to even look at the car. The investigation was a sham put on for the sake of a grieving father. Heidi was just another little girl to the world. What they did not understand, she *was* the world to her Daddy and the brutal truth was that none of the authorities cared enough to do anything about it.

The trained eye of the investigator found that debris filled the latch portion of the seat belt and that was the first piece of evidence to show the seat belt was not fastened. Haydon was sitting in his car seat, with his seat belt on and the seat belt latch was clean. Checking Heather's seat belt in the driver seat, the latch was clean. Her seat belt had been cut to release her as it was still attached when the paramedics arrived. Both belts were extended which was also proof they had been used, the center seat and back left seat belts were both still rolled up in the holder and both latches were full of glass and other debris. Larry's heart sank. His daughter could have lived if she had had her seat belt on. Heidi would have been sitting in the center seat, of which she always did. This was not just an accident, she did not have on her seat belt, and that reverberated over and over in his head. Heidi would still be alive; yes, she may have been hurt but not killed. Where in the reports was this to be found? Did no one care?

Terrifying Memories

Why did Heidi not have her seat belt fastened? The only person willing and able to answer that question was her brother Haydon. Do you dare ask him and bring up terrifying memories? Larry discussed it with his counselor and decided it was up to Haydon. If he wanted to talk and tell the police what happened he would, if not they would not push it. The police came to the house to talk to Haydon and the following is a brief recount of what happened that day.

That morning was like any other, they left for school with Haydon in his car seat and Heidi sitting in the middle seat. Both buckled in. Heidi was playing with a toy and Haydon was playing with a toy as they started out for a normal day. Heidi wanted to get to school early as she was excited about the SAT 9 testing. Haydon told the heart-wrenching story of dropping his toy on the floor of the car. Heidi's mother told her to un-buckle her seat belt and pick up the toy for Haydon. Before she could re-buckle her seat belt the car struck the truck throwing Heidi into the accident. Haydon told the story slowly and quietly.

Haydon, the Survivor

A Child and Fear

Haydon is such a loving little boy full of excitement and wonder, how he loved his sister Heidi. Haydon suffered from severe Post Traumatic Stress (PTS) after the accident. He shared so much with his sister and for such a young child to witness her death, how would he ever handle this? Children are so resilient and some find a way to store the information and get through the moment. He was torn between two parents wanting and needing both to insure his survival, his emotional survival. His dad gave him the freedom to share his most awful thoughts and memories and assured him of his love daily. I recall a couple of days after the accident Haydon was playing catch with grandpa. Usually a great catch, he missed a ball thrown to him. Immediately he had meltdown and started crying that grandpa could have killed him if the ball hit his head. Months would pass before he could ride in a car without telling us to be careful, watch out for the other car, and drive slower. If we ever had to put the breaks on fast, Haydon would remark, "Be careful you almost got us in an accident, I could die." How can a five-year old possibly process this scene in his mind?

Haydon had been with us since he was one. He learned to walk and run, swim, and play ball while living with us. Like his sister, Haydon excelled in sports. He accomplished riding a two-wheel bike early, and the faster he could go the better. He played hard and slept deep. He loved playing tickle tummy with Daddy, reading books and praying together. Haydon noticed everything around him. He could tell you what the person that helped you at the check out counter was wearing and usually comment on it. Interestingly enough, Haydon is colorblind.

Haydon had overcome serious surgery at the age of three. Overnight a growth had appeared on his neck. At first, it was thought to be the mumps, but after a visit to the doctors he was diagnosed with cystic hygroma, defined by the medical dictionary as; "A lesion caused by a mass of dilated lymphatics, due to the failure of the embryonic lymphatics to connect with the venous system." It's a birth defect that usually develops on the side of the neck. Whatever the cause, we all were frightened. I knew God was there with us the entire way. We prayed daily for a healing of Haydon.

At first the doctors thought is was a tumor and Haydon was admitted to the hospital for several days trying to drain or reduce the size of the growth but it continued to enlarge. In May of 2000 after several attempts to reduce the growth, surgery was performed. Larry had been told it was extremely delicate and could result in the loss of muscles to his shoulder and tongue with the possibility of a droopy lip, which would affect his speech.

The doctors had asked for blood to be donated as the surgery was in the neck area and they were not sure what they would find once the surgery had begun. Larry had just recovered from a cold and they would not allow him to give blood. As both he and Haydon have O negative blood types, it would have been the easy thing to do. Our prayers were to find a blood donor. We put the word out to friends to see if anyone could donate blood. There were two donors that came forward. Both were out of town and gave of their time to travel substantial distances to give blood the week before Haydon's surgery.

Haydon had had two separate stays in the hospital. Larry would spend the night as often as possible. We would take all of the cousins and Heidi to visit and bring him movies and toys. Haydon had an attitude that was truly amazing. He rarely cried and wanted to be strong, he was a brave little boy at three. When the surgery was complete, we were all informed it was a cyst, not a tumor and there would be no residual affects on his muscles. There were, however, two problems resulting from the surgery. Haydon lost his front teeth three years too soon because the clamps, which were used to hold his mouth open during surgery, were too tight. As a result his speech development has been slower than normal.

Haydon is loving, smart, outgoing and has the same great sense of humor his sister had. He strives to please his mom and dad; he loves them both so deeply. This little boy will have many challenges in his life as a result of this tragedy at such a young age. I believe God knew the road Haydon was to walk and as he grows, God will guide his path and wherever that path may go, whatever journey he will be led on, God will turn his pain into something wonderful, something good.

Trusting the System or Trusting God

Actions and Consequences

Larry took the pictures and report, along with the investigator, to the Orange County DA and showed him what they found. They went over the re-interviews of the witnesses and found that Heather was probably looking in the rearview mirror at the time of the accident to see if Heidi was following her instructions, therefore, not even seeing the truck. She only responded when Haydon yelled at his mother to, "Move Mommy move" and it was too late. After reviewing the new information, the DA agreed with them on their findings including the fact that Heidi did not have on her seat belt fastened. However, Larry quickly found out how the system works. The DA had budget cuts that year and it would not be politically correct or financially responsible to prosecute a mother who has lost her only daughter due to her own negligence. It would not be a popular case and it was not up to the DA to issue a citation, that was up to the police. Not only was the DA not going to do anything, it was left up to the police to correct the report, to do what was right. Both the policeman and the fireman that had filed reports were confronted and stood firm on what they saw and wrote, via other people, she was buckled in and sitting behind her mother.

Larry pleaded with them to look at the pictures, to

go look at the car and they all refused. If either of these men had any integrity, there would have been no question and the reports would have been corrected. They feared what would happen if they changed these reports; being reprimanded by their superiors for filing incorrect reports and not following procedure. "Trust the system, let it work for you." These were empty words spoken by men of little character, fearful men, men who have grown hard in the realities of the flesh. I truly doubt they would have received any reprimand but that is what Larry was told in an effort to get him to *go away*. Their own fear for self outweighed what was right, with this decision they each decided the truth would never be told to anyone, not even a little boy who would one day want to know the truth about his sister's death. These police and fire officials decided to deny the truth and affect the future of this little boy. I lost a great deal of respect for our law enforcement that day.

With this meeting Larry knew deep in the recess of his heart nothing was going to happen. The reports would never be corrected; there would be no ticket or punishment for Heather. The system is not interested in responsibility or consequence or justice unless it brings attention from the press and advances political agendas. Justice for the average person is not available for we are not politically correct, we have no political strength. This cover-up was of little consequence to the world, but world shattering to all of us.

What did we all want to come from this? Did we want Haydon's mother to go to jail? No, we just wanted someone to establish responsibility, someone to raise their hand and say "I messed up, please forgive me." We all wanted something as a consequence in a society that has no consequences. We wanted closure of which there was none.

Something Is Better Than Nothing

A few weeks later Heather's driver's license was suspended, as is the law when you are in an accident that results in a death. The law states the suspension would last for one year; however, you do have the right to appeal the suspension. This would be the consequence Larry had hoped for, or so he thought. The appeal was handled without Larry being notified. The father of the child killed would have no say so in the appeal process. Again God works in amazing ways.

A staff member had to go for her license renewal and while sitting and waiting to be called for her appointment; the attorney sitting next to her responded to a call, "All parties here for the Heather Nix appeal." If this had not happened, Larry would have not known about the appeal. Upon the appeal, her driver's license was returned, no further consequence, no accountability, life just goes on, and to the world it was just an accident.

Shattered Lives

The Holidays

Before we knew it Thanksgiving was here, we had the family or what was left of it over for dinner. Tony did not come to dinner. Before dinner, we all lit a candle in memory of Heidi. We all ate, sat quietly and the day was over. Life went on in a fog that was growing thicker and deeper. Christmas came, and oh, how difficult that was. Each time I entered a store to buy for the other children, I was reminded of Heidi. It would only take seeing a Roxy outfit and I was brought to tears. Larry told of going shopping and having to leave the store in tears as his heart broke knowing he would never buy for his daughter again. This year was Larry's time to have Haydon on Christmas Eve, so our Christmas with all of the children was on that evening.

Christmas dinner was to be at Michelle's along with Tony's family. Something out of the ordinary, something we thought would take away the memories, the pain. It was raining heavy that day and Larry went to the cemetery and spent several hours sitting in the rain. No head stone just a piece of grass growing over the fresh earth. I imagined he sat there crying as the rain ran down his face, alone. How could he participate in the Christmas festivities when Heidi was gone, his life, and his future gone? How could any of us have left him alone? Yet each family member was hurting and alone, even with a group of people standing around.

We had not put anything on Heidi's grave for the holiday season, no flowers, no tree. Everyday as I drove to work, I thought about putting something on her grave but my mind and the activities around the holidays would pull me away to something else. It was easy to be pulled away from doing something hard. Again, with hindsight, it was too difficult for me to embrace the reality of this Christmas without Heidi.

Larry grew very angry with us for not putting a remembrance on her grave. All of the other graves had Christmas trees and decorations. Nothing was adorning Heidi's grave. He so wanted us to put something there, to show we remembered not just Heidi, but also his pain, his feelings, to put him first. The rain continued on through the day, it felt so appropriate; God was crying and grieving for us. He saw our brokenness and He wept. The following day, Larry Sr. and I took flowers and placed them on her grave and we cried, alone. Standing there together, each alone with our pain, our fear. The holiday's came and went as the clouds of depression pressed in on all of us, hard, stifling.

The First Birthday

Heidi's birthday came in March. We took flowers to the gravesite that afternoon and cried. Crying was an everyday occurrence, a ritual of passage. On this important day we made sure to place flowers on Heidi's grave. It was not only to remember her but it was a way to let Larry know we did not forget his pain. As hard as it was I would embrace the pain and go to her grave and be present in the moment. Michelle, Tony and the children went to the gravesite and released nine balloons in honor of her ninth birthday. As Larry Sr. and I were leaving, Larry and Haydon showed up to have lunch at the gravesite. They would sit and talk and cry together. Larry shared his soul with Haydon.

I have never been a grave visitor. It seemed to me a senseless act, as I believe the person I loved so deeply is not there, only the tent they lived in while here on earth is there. I recently went back to my father's grave to see what was on his headstone. He died in May of 2000 and I had not been back until recently. I suppose that does not say much about me. I went to my mother's grave once to make sure the head stone was correct and returned on the day we buried my father. This year (2005) on Mother's Day I took flowers to my mother's grave, I cried, how I miss her, especially now.

Maybe there is something in me that makes that visit too difficult emotionally. Admitting the need I had for the person who is gone, admitting my attachment, admitting my pain, admitting my loss, admitting my need of God so desperately; how I ran from this for most of my life. I have taken a closer look at my feelings about visiting a loved ones grave to the point that now, when I visit Heidi's grave, sadness overtakes me like a wave crashing down but I am also reminded of the wonderful blessing she was and is in my life. I am reminded of why I am here and how much I want to live my life for Christ so I will one day be re-united with this beautiful little girl.

Divorce

March arrives; in like a lion out like a lamb. Tony walked into my office and quit, he had had enough, could not nor did not want to cope any longer. He wanted out of everything as quickly as possible. He went and picked up Dylan from baseball practice, the kids from day care and took them home frightened and crying. He sat them down, told them their parents were getting a divorce, and he would be moving out as soon as he got a job and a place to live. Michelle walked into a scene of crying children and violent anger. She was frightened. I am not sure Michelle really ever thought he would leave; her reality was something and somewhere else at that time, it had to be any place other than with Tony or she could not survive. She and the children came to our home to seek refuge and comfort. Larry was there giving neither. He had to take care of himself and could not afford giving up his fencing project. Michelle and the children spent the night, and returned to their home the next night with Tony still there.

Tony moved out March 15th, one week after Heidi's birthday. Each day and night was strewn with the seeds of anger and emotional upheaval, and the soil of bitterness took those seeds and grew them into bitter roots. Tony had to leave if these children were to survive. The seeds of hatred were being placed in their hearts and minds and fed by the bitterness of each parent. He had to leave for anyone to survive and Michelle told him so. He moved in with his mother for a couple of months.

He continued, for the remainder of the year, not to pay child support or offer financial help to Michelle and the children in any way. He knew his in-laws well; he knew we would help her at any cost, because of the children. We could not stand by and watch these children lose any more. Maybe it was us who could not stand to lose any more. Maybe we needed to learn how to build a fence to protect our property, our souls. How do you say no in a crisis, where do you draw the line, when is helping not helping?

Whose Fault Is It Anyway?

Tony became the ultimate victim, with the inability to take responsibility for any of his actions. He had sunk to the depths of not having control over anything in his life, except pointing. Pointing out who was at fault, the other person and mostly Michelle, what Michelle should do, file bankruptcy and sell the house, pointing out he had no money; it was not his fault he quit his job, that was entirely my fault.

Michelle was not without fault; she had helped create this monster with her own baggage from her family, from me. They both brought together bags of dysfunction, unrealistic expectations of marriage and the inability to set boundaries. A prescription for a disastrous marriage, one only God would be able to heal. The problem was these two individuals would have to reach out to God, together, get on their knees and ask for help together. That would not happen, pride was too strong, they were each strong in their self, they would handle this situation their self and their way.

Michelle was crying out to God for a healing of her marriage, but sometimes our pain is a result of our previous choices. When we find ourselves in the midst of a crisis we cry out for God's help. The only problem: God did not lead us into our difficulty, we did that on our own, yet we want Him to rescue us. Oh, the regrets, how many times in my life have I experienced the desperation and fear of realizing I messed up, again. When I decided to do things my way, then when I would crash and burn, the cries would immediately go out to God for His help. These are roads we all must travel in life, valleys we visit and learn from, alone with God. Yes, I said *alone with God,* for our faith develops when we spend time *alone* with God. He does not leave us, we are the ones that pull away, walk away. God does not leave us, never, even when we mess up and God did not leave Michelle.

Tony was resenting Michelle's time at church and did not understand where God fit into his marriage. He had never had to deal with God before and he was not about to start now. With God in the picture Tony felt he had no control and that was something he needed desperately to get back.

We never need help to destroy ourselves, that is something we do well on our own and Satan is more than happy to assist our efforts. He is always willing to show us the path to destruction. We can destroy marriages and lives with little help once we block God out. We need help to heal, forgive and grow and that help only comes from God. I have found in life you do not have to accept that fact, you do not have to accept God's guidance, God's word, God's laws, but they are always the same, always there. They are like gravity, it is always here and always working whether you believe in it or not.

Every special day came and went with a sense of being frozen, frozen from feelings, tears pouring out and freezing on my face. It seemed nothing was ever right, so I stayed numb. I felt like a jack-in-the-box, constantly jumping up to fill a need for Larry, Michelle and Larry Sr. The feeling to keep busy was overwhelming, I had to keep busy, and I had to stay numb, so numb. One crisis after another, death, loss, abandonment, fear, grief and it went on and on. One step at a time, one day at a time, one crisis at a time, staying numb was good.

Business Must Go On

On top of this emotional turmoil was the task of running a business, or should I say the business was running itself. The staff was doing a great job at doing what they do day in and day out. But keeping a business healthy is an ongoing task requiring much more than just the daily tasks of opening the doors and answering the phone. You have to sell product and services; you have to plant seeds to reap the harvest and the process must continue year after year.

Leading a business requires emotional effort and I had none left to give. Yes, I went through the motions every day. I handled all the crises that arose, and there were many. I talked to people day in and day out, always guarding my feelings, never letting anyone get too close to the raw nerves. Fearing if any one got too close I would break down and not be able to pull myself back, always guarded. I was not able to focus on one thought for very long. Each day I would take one-step forward and then fall down. I kept trying to keep myself centered on something, on anything. After all, it was my place to pick up the pieces and carry my family, right? Yet, every night, alone, quietly, I would fall apart.

The business was not doing well and I knew it. It was going to take some drastic changes to survive. I was not ready to even handle the daily activities of the business much less implement drastic changes. I prayed for wisdom, discernment and energy to do whatever must be done. The answer was a band-aid and it came in the form of an Equity Line of credit on our home. This was the first time we ever put the security of our personal property in the business. This band-aid was not the long term answer and I knew it and the bleeding continued.

A Life Time in One Year

The First Anniversary

As the first anniversary of Heidi's death approached it was like I had lived an entire life time and death was near, but for some reason life was still going on but it was without me in it. We had talked about what to do for this anniversary and could not agree on anything except that we did not want to be where we were. Some friends of Larry's took it in their hands and planned the morning and evening events to remember and honor Heidi. Larry and some friends met Graydon Jessup, the Senior Pastor at Eastside Christian Church, at the accident site in the morning, at the exact time of her death. Larry wanted to be there at that specific time. In our mind the entire last year was so unreal. If we only had a time machine we could relive the accident, we could stop what had happened. We desperately wanted to create a new world where this tragedy would all have been a dream. Our life would return to the way it was and we would walk over to the car and give Heidi a big hug. Yet we knew deep down this would not happen and this day offered only the beginning of a hard acceptance of what was now our reality. It was like a slap on the face to wake you up and you realize nothing in the way of consequence or accountability was going to happen, that your life was going to continue and you better find a way to deal with this reality. I had the option to continue being numb or choose to start feeling again. I could choose to let God work it out or I could continue to try and do it myself.

Sometimes when you have been numb for so long, when you start the feeling process it is very painful and so it would be here. It was like sitting with your legs crossed for an extended period of time and then standing up. The weakness and the rush of blood to those nerves that have been cut off for so long become almost too painful to use again. I had to stand and face the pain: I knew that in my head, yet when I awoke each morning, numb looked good. Everything seemed so unreal, like I was watching a movie; I was so unattached to this whole process. For the day I chose numb, it seemed a safer place to be.

That evening approximately 45 people attended a candle light memorial at the accident site. We were all reminded nothing was to be placed at the site of the accident. The person living at the house on the corner did not want anyone placing reminders of this little girl's death. It was too upsetting for her, so she took a stand and made it known by removing any flowers that people would place there. I had placed some plants there months before and they had promptly been removed. It happened that a teacher lived in this house and had planted flowers at the site of the accident in an effort to curtail anyone else putting flowers and reminders at this site. We were told of her care to select special flowers, however, the flowers that meant something special to this teacher, meant nothing to us, to Larry. We so wanted to show the world, in our way, of our love for Heidi by showering a place that brought up awful memories with piles of flowers and candles, something that meant something to all of us who attended. This person did not even walk out her door to acknowledge this memorial. She had also been hit with the ripples from this tragedy. Not knowing what to do or say to us, her needs became primary. Again it became about someone other than Larry and his need, his grief. He was again denied the process that he so desperately needed, the ability to stand where Heidi once was alive and turn a nightmare into a sweet memory. Denied this expression of love, we stood across the street with candles telling stories about Heidi and lifting up a prayer for healing and forgiveness.

There was such a need to forgive. The forgiveness was not just for others. I struggled to understand the actions of others, yet could not always explain my own actions. I knew God wanted me to forgive and the forgiveness had to start by forgiving myself.

> *"Do not let any unwholesome talk come out of your mouths, but only what is helpful for building others up according to their needs, that it may benefit those who listen. . . . Get rid of all bitterness, rage and anger, brawling and slander, along with every form of malice. Be kind and compassionate to one another, forgiving each other, just as in Christ God forgave you." Ephesians 4:29–32 (NIV)*

I know these words, I believe these words, I trust the truth of God's words, and I must live these words. Even when numb, they resonate in my mind, there must be a way God will restore my heart and I will again embrace this truth. The night ended with a visit to Larry's friend's home where we talked and laughed about nothing of importance. The night ended numb.

Building Up and Falling Apart

Turning Fences into Walls

Larry traveled to Utah a week or so after the first anniversary of Heidi's death. Originally it was intended for me to travel with him. As the time approached, his anger grew. He was pounding each fence post into the ground, building his protection. At first I thought it was something I had done wrong, something I had said. It was neither. It was his pain, his fear, building up deep down trying to come out and face what his reality was to be. What he had pushed aside for a year, he now had to face and it would be harder than he ever imagined. He needed desperately to protect his property, his soul and this was how it would be.

He went on his trip and everything went well. Larry had a need to stop at the gas station where he received the life changing call. He called to let me know where he was, I could hear the pain in his voice, the tears held back. It was a connection we would always share, that life changing moment. He continued on his trip and it was, in business terms, successful.

He arrived home late in the afternoon. Larry Sr. and I had gone out to dinner and upon walking into the house, the roof fell in. I do not remember what even started the conversation; I only remember the venom that came spewing out of his mouth. By the end of the conversation, Larry and his father were yelling vulgar remarks at each other. What had happened? What went wrong? I knew this was something I could not fix. Larry was pounding in more stakes and expanding his property. We were getting too close, and it was not good for him to be too close to anyone, that was too scary.

The days continued and the stress between us was growing like mold on a wet wall. There was no light, I saw no hope, and we all felt the ugly mold growing. As the ugliness inched its way along the lining of our soul it began to take our breath away, our life away, one day at a time. I continued to pray and pray day in and day out for God to intervene, to heal our family. I begged for mercy, "Where are you God? I need you, my family needs you, please help us." God said, "Wait."

I Give You My Life

End of May came and we had a trade show to attend in Seattle, Washington. Larry Sr. and I decided to go early, as it was our anniversary and this would give us some time alone. We met our friends from Texas there and spent a week seeing the sights. Each day was a struggle for me to focus on the *fun* we were having. I tried so hard to look at the beauty around me and embrace the life I had. Why was emptiness overwhelming me? I spent a couple of days in the room alone. I wanted to be quiet and alone, just to read and write. I could have stayed in the room for the week and not missed a thing but I felt guilty about letting Larry Sr. down. He so wanted to go through the motions of living again. It was all I could do not to cry continuously. It was a relief when we reached the day to go to the trade show. That meant only four days left before I could go home. Maybe this time home would be ok. The mold would be gone, the fence torn down; I knew in the deep recesses of my heart it would not be, but at least at home I did not have to put on a happy face, a pretend face. I could be the ugly me I wanted to be.

Larry flew into town the day before the trade show was to start. We drove to the airport and picked him up, he checked into his room and we did not see him until the day of the show and then saw him only during show hours. The fence was almost complete, he was withdrawn and alone, he looked lost. He was lost, his daughter was gone, and he was so lost. Another post pounded into the ground and cemented in.

I recall a conversation during the show where Larry casually asked me if it would be a problem for his dad and me to take our names off of the deed on a condominium we shared ownership in. I told him it was not a big deal to me and did not believe it would be to his dad. Nothing more said. I did not think much of it until later.

When you are grieving and your thought process is impaired, it is not a good idea to build fences. Especially ones with no gate and ones so high no one can see in and so wide no one can reach you. A high fence becomes a wall and walls have a tendency to isolate you. Isolation in grief only creates more fear and that fear drives us deeper into the darkness. With a wall and no door you have no way of letting the pain out that you took in with you. The pain begins to eat at your heart, at your soul. Your goal is to keep hurt out but with no entrance or exit, there is also no escape. You shut out any possible good God wants to give you. Protecting your property is good, but you have to realize doors are needed in life. They allow good to come in and we can shut them to keep danger out.

The show came and went with little said between the three of us. We all stayed away from each other as much as possible. We could not bare a confrontation, not here, not at a trade show when you are on stage all day and all night. There were times I felt like the leper walking the streets of Jerusalem and everyone running away not wanting to get near. I felt it would have been easier if I yelled while I walked around, "Leper, leper, stay a way, do not come close or you will reap the harvest of brokenness and death." I did not want to become the victim, I did not want to be "poor me." I had reached a time to decide, live or go deeper into the darkness. I prayed every day for relief, for light, for hope. "Dear God, show me Your will, Your way. I give You my life." It was time; it was up to me to choose what my life was to be like from this day forward.

Off the Tracks

We returned home from the trade show with great anticipation and the growing need of new business. I came back with the excitement of starting from this day forward to live again. I had mentioned to Larry Sr. the question Larry had asked about our names on the deed. He came back at me with disdain, how could I have asked such a thing? How could Larry have the nerve to ask such a thing? He was adamant about not taking his name off the deed and he would take that stand at any cost. I did not understand and thought he would change his mind in time. Larry Sr. did not even talk to Larry about why or what this was all about.

In my great success with triangulation, I carried the message from one person to the other. Never really filling in all of the blanks, because at this stage in my life blanks were details and I did not have the emotional capacity to concern myself with details. The more blanks the better. If you wanted to know, go ask for yourself. Well, that did not happen, as Larry Sr. could not risk the verbal attack, and did not want to deal with the truth about his relationship with his son. He chose to continue viewing their relationship as wonderful on his best delusional day. Delusion has a way of creating its own life and it will swallow you up quickly if left un-attended.

About a week after returning from Seattle, Larry asked me at work if his dad was going to sign over the condominium. I told him he needed to talk with his dad, that he did not want to take his name off the deed. I was never given the chance to discuss or complete my sentence, which was all it took. Within an hour, Larry was moving out, wanted nothing to do with his family. We were all liars, we were all sick, we cared nothing about him, we meant nothing to him, and he was going to sue us.

From that point on, our relationship has been strained, distant, broken. The train we all got on to run away had run off the tracks and each car had plunged into the icy waters of anger. Larry had completed his fence and there was no gate. Within two weeks Larry and Haydon moved out, we never got to say goodbye to Haydon and to this day I do not know Larry's exact address He wants nothing to do with us except at work when he must communicate with me. We are inconsequential to him, we are thieves, liars, and frauds and his words cut deep and hurt terribly. Larry had reached his breaking point. It was decided without any further discussion and it appeared the process of divorcing his family came as quickly as his divorce from his wife. In reality, the process had taken years and had been accelerated by Heidi's death. The pus was oozing, the hurt, the physical pain; the grief all appeared as anger. No looking back, no reconciliation, no more talking, no more chances.

"God, what have I done wrong? Are we being punished? Show me Lord, oh, Lord help this hurting family."

Fenced Off and Walled In

I begged Larry Sr. to change his mind about the condominium but he refused. It became a sticking point and he would not change. In my mind, he put money in front of his relationship with his son. In his mind he finally stood up to his son and said no. We had gone for 13 months of putting everyone before Larry at a time he needed us desperately. I can say today we were unable to get outside our own hurt and pain and we were mentally unable to help him any more than we did. We could not help ourselves. It had been all about our feelings and us. It had been about survival. It had been about me wanting to fix everything. It had been about Larry Sr. and his pain. Not once had we sat down and listened to Larry and heard his pain, shared his grief or held him while he cried.

Our minister talked to Larry Sr. but he would not change his mind. I felt as if someone had torn my body in half, wanting so desperately to keep my connection with both my husband and son, not wanting another loss, another crisis. Had I been walking a fence between the two of them? If so, the fence had collapsed and I was thrown down hard to the ground. When thrown to the ground, God is giving you the opportunity to get on your knees and reach out to Him and pray for the strength and wisdom to stand again. As I lay there crushed, I realized if anyone was going to pick me up, hold me up, it would be God. He was my constant help and fortress.

> *"Praise be to the Lord, for he has heard my cry for mercy. The lord is my strength and my shield; my heart trusts in him, and I am helped." Psalm 28:6–7a (NIV)*

A Little Child Will Lead Them

We had no way of getting in touch with Larry, even by phone. He did not want anyone to know where he lived. He was fenced off physically and emotionally. He would make it on his own or not at all, this was the way it should be in his eyes. It was about a month before we saw Haydon again and that was because he would wake up crying and wanting to know why he could not see us, especially his grandpa. We had been a very important part of Haydon's life. Haydon had lived with us most of his life. The sudden change of residence with no discussion between Haydon and us made it difficult. It was not only a loss and an emotional adjustment for us, but also one for Haydon. He had lost a sister and now had lost his grandparents. We had lost a granddaughter and now our grandson. We had all been a large part of each others lives. Again God stepped in and directed several lives.

> *"The wolf will live with the lamb, the leopard will lie down with the goat, the calf and the lion and the yearling together; and a little child will lead them." Isaiah 11:6 (NIV)*

Haydon felt free to tell his mother about his feelings and about missing his grandpa. She asked if he would like to call and see if grandpa would come pick him up for a visit. He wanted to make sure we were ok and wanted to spend some time with us. Both Haydon and his mother did not want us to tell Larry we were seeing Haydon. The relationship was already split and I did not want it to be any deeper, it wasn't right not to tell Larry. We needed to honor Larry's request no matter how painful those requests may be. Larry was traveling again and I called his cell phone and left a message asking if it was ok for us to see Haydon as he had called wanting to see us. His answer was; "I don't care what Heather does on her days." We continue to see Haydon when he calls, usually on his mother's days.

Teach me to do Your Will

Restoring What is Left

To this day my husband and I continue on in counseling, wanting and working to restore what is left of our life, to build our relationship into one of meaning with a stronger foundation. It is like starting all over from the ground up and is not easy. I have spent two years finding out how to get through grief and in the process finding myself along with God's purpose for my life.

> "Teach me to do your will, for you are my God; may your good Spirit lead me on level ground." Psalm 143:10 (NIV)

I have made it through the valley and am starting to climb the mountain. Feelings have come back to me and I am able to distinguish between the important and not so important things in life. I have little time for small talk, and enjoy deep conversations and deep books and quiet times at home. I treasure our friends and family more than ever. I view the sunrise and sunset as a reminder of the promises from God. I notice the birds more and the children at play more. I notice who my grandchildren are becoming, each unique, each a special creation of God. I see their special gifts and encourage them to find their purpose. The small things are important; my senses seem to be more heightened. God continues working in my life for I am His work in process and He is never changing.

> *"Jesus Christ is the same yesterday and today and forever." Hebrews 13:8 (NIV)*

I know there will continue to be challenges in my life, difficulties to overcome. I stand on God's promises continually.

> *"No one will be able to stand up against you all the days of your life. As I was with Moses, so I will be with you; I will never leave you nor forsake you." Joshua 1:5 (NIV)*

Trusting God in Business

The jury is still out on our business and we continue to struggle. I trusted God twenty-five years ago when we started this business, and I will continue trusting Him for guidance as we plant our seeds. My faith is strong and I expect a harvest beyond measure; one to show the power of God and His promises. Only God knows what will happen and I am at peace with that. I trust Him daily for our daily bread and know He will supply what we need for that day in every way. The business has been on hold for the past two years as God has been working very hard on me, yet I trust God has a plan there also and when the time is right it will be revealed.

> *"'For I know the plans I have for you', declares the Lord,' plans to prosper you and not to harm you, plans to give you hope and a future. Then you will call upon me and come and pray to me, and I will listen to you. You will seek*

> *me and find me when you seek me with all your heart.' "*
> *Jeremiah 29:11–13 (NIV)*

Is it easy? No, and I struggle in my prideful way to take back control of my life and try to fix everything. My morning time with God reminds me He is in charge and can handle my life better than I can. So I stay on my knees and on my face in prayer.

> *"Train a child in the way he should go, and when he is old he will not turn from it." Proverbs 22:6 (NIV)*

Michelle has gone through a difficult divorce and is attempting to hold her life together with her children. Her journey will continue to have many twists and turns, ups and downs. She will continue to have the challenges of single parenthood. Her financial difficulties are continuing. I believe God allows us to hurt and go through difficulties to grow our faith and to help us learn what our priorities should be. He will let us go to the point of financial failure if that is what it takes to reach us and to get us *home.* God has her on a journey to mold and shape her into the person He wants her to be and I am sure she will continue on kicking and fighting the whole way, but continue she will. Her road will be a different one from mine, as it should be. She has struggled to pull away as we have struggled to let her go and become the independent person God wants to use. God wants to use us as individuals for we are saved as individuals, not as attachments to our parents or children. Our identity and worth is not to be connected to our children or our parents, only to God. This too is a process we are working on, letting go and setting healthy boundaries, and we will.

> *"He will turn the hearts of the fathers to their children, and the hearts of the children to their fathers."* Malachi 4:6a (NIV)

Larry continues to pull each fiber of his being away. One thread at a time each bleeding and torn, each painful as it is pulled out like an arrow that has been shot into his heart. As the arrow is pulled out, it tears the flesh and we bleed, but it must be pulled out to heal. His grief has magnified each past hurt and those hurts have become infected with anger. As each hurtful arrow is pulled out, it has sprayed the infection all over each one of us. That happens in families, even strong families. There have been small windows with rays of hope open; maybe he is beginning to install a gate, and I pray he will let God build it for him. God is working a mighty work in Larry's life; he will have a great testimony if he listens to the urgings of Holy Spirit and allows God to direct his path. Larry had to pull away because we were holding on too tight, wanting to fix and control his life. Breaking away from us was not a bad thing; we made it a hard and hurtful process. Letting go of our children is both sweet and painful, it is God's plan. I must be like the mother bird, nudge them away so they can develop their wings. Only then can they soar like the eagles God intended them to be. Larry will soar, he will overcome, and he will love again because God will never leave his side.

The Strongest Piece of the Puzzle

With all of the pain, grief, hurt, and difficulties that have gone on and continue to go on in my family I trust God will restore us. For our family possesses the strongest piece of the puzzle in life, Love.

"Love is patient, love is kind. It does not envy, it does not boast, it is not proud. It is not rude, it is not self-seeking, it is not easily angered, it keeps on record of wrongs. Love does not delight in evil but rejoices with the truth. It always protects, always trusts, always hopes, always preserves. Love never fails. But where there are prophecies, they will cease; where there are tongues, they will be stilled; where there is knowledge, it will pass away. For we know in part and we prophesy in part, but when perfection comes, the imperfect disappears. When I was a child, I talked like a child; I thought like a child, I reasoned like a child. When I became a man, I put childish ways behind me. Now we see but a poor reflection as in a mirror; then we shall see face to face. Now I know in part; then I shall know fully, even as I am fully known. And now these three remain: faith, hope and love. But the greatest of these is love." I Corinthians 13: 4–13 (NIV)

Your Journey

Traveling Down Your Road

Grief and loss are powerful emotions; don't underestimate what they can do in and to your life. Many times we fall before we can stand, before we reach new heights in our life. Sharing your true thoughts and feelings with your loved ones, your friends and family, is so important in returning to a healthy life. If they do not nor cannot walk this road with you find someone who can, a pastor or counselor.

Grief may take you on a journey that is long and hard and if you accept the journey, you can find love and change and grow through the experience. You may find the changes will take you to the mountaintop. I have to remind myself that God did not make mountains without valleys in between. As you travel down this road there will be many forks, many choices. Look to embrace all of the thoughts and emotions that come in this process. For when you embrace your feelings, you will be running toward God and embracing Him as He gave you these feelings; He has felt what you are feeling. Don't deny them, don't cover them up, feel them, know them, for then you will know yourself and only then can you let the pain go.

Look to God for direction, trust Him completely, continue to pray for guidance and give it time. Remember, God's time is not our time and grief does not have a clock. Grief fits into no one's schedule. Loss and grief are part of our life's journey and just like joy and happiness it is to be shared and embraced. God has given us the gift of the Holy Spirit to be with us both on the mountaintops and in the valleys and to help us rise above it all and to hold our hand as we journey *home*.

And our journey continues . . .

Heidi Heaven Bound

We hadn't any warning
The day it all went mad.
We knew not yet of quicksand,
Or lives like shattered glass.

The day was drenched in beauty,
The sky was blue and bright.
Everything was in its order,
Life's direction was clear and right.

Our business day was starting
Our return home was set and planned
Then an unexpected phone call
That caused our breath to end.

The sky turned dark, we grasped for air
The shock, the tears, the unbelief
This cannot happen, oh dear God,
My Heidi girl she is gone.

The shaking so intense inside,
How do I tell her brother?
Eight years old too soon to die
My reason for life why bother?

The long flight home in such distress
We reach our family, hug and cry.
Our Heidi, our Girlie, she is gone
We did not even say goodbye.

How long this forever
Heidi's death and our lives
The sadness, the anger
How do we survive?

God reached down that day
And held Heidi's hand
I have no doubt her entrance
To heaven was above all grand.

Though Heidi is gone from us forever
And we long to see her face
Not one minute of her living
Could her death ever replace.

Though my body quivers and quakes
I rejoice in her short life
My Angel from Heaven may be gone from earth
My Heidi lives on in God's eternal light.

Marsha Nix

Heidi's Head Stone

Heidi Nicole Nix
March 9, 1995–April 29, 2003
A blessing in the lives of those she touched.
Heidi mad a difference, a beautiful difference.
A smile
A long hug
A kiss goodnight
Heidi looked at people and saw love.
Those who knew Heidi looked at her and saw an Angel.

"Let the little children come to me, and do not hinder them, for the kingdom of heaven belongs to such as these." Matthew 19:14

Epilogue

When I started writing this book I had been thrown to the ground and was facing my Red Sea experience. I had death, loss, hurt, depression and darkness coming at me from behind. In front was a sea of devastating emotions, loneliness, grief, and unbearable pain. I could not turn back for there would be no coming out of that hole, I would be a slave to depression for the rest of my life. Yet how was I to go forward as I stood looking at the sea, so big, so wide and so very deep. Only God could part the waters, only God could move the mountain and He did through prayer and this book.

It started out as something that would be part of my healing process, and that was all. Yet as the words poured out it became clear this was supposed to be something else, something to touch others, something to touch my broken family and something to reach out to the hurting, the grieving. Was this to be my purpose?

I finished writing the first manuscript in early March 2005. Our family was torn and there was no sight of reconciliation. The prompting of the Holy Spirit is something that you cannot always explain yet that is what it was, a prompting. When the Holy Spirit speaks, listen, and that is exactly what I did. I printed out the pages of the first manuscript and gave it to my husband to read, not even sure he would spend the time and effort to read it. Apprehension was setting in; everyone would think this is crazy maybe I should just leave it alone. It was after dinner one evening when I offered up my heart.

"Larry, I finished my book. Do you want to read it?"

I received a nonchalant reply, "I guess so." I laid it on the table and went to bed.

God works in amazing ways. In the morning I found Larry Sr. had stayed up most of the night reading and crying through the book. These words that had poured out of my heart had touched him and reopened wounds that had yet to heal. He read about my feelings of which he had no previous knowledge, because we did not share the scary stuff. He relived the hurt of Michelle and Tony's divorce and was left still not understanding. He read about and understood Larry's pain and the hole in his heart in a whole new light.

I decided to give the book to my children to read, maybe to relieve my guilt, maybe just to share my heart. Whatever the reason, it was a prompting of the Holy Spirit.

The first was Michelle: "I wrote a book about Heidi and our families' experience. Do you want to read it? If there is anything you want to be removed let me know, I may submit it to be published."

Her quick uninterested reply, "Sure, I'll read it."

It took her a couple of weeks before she even picked up the manuscript. After reading it, Michelle gave the manuscript back with the comment; "Why would anyone want to read about our dysfunctional family?"

The next day I was prompted again by the Holy Spirit to give the book to Larry, this would be the most difficult one for me. Our relationship was broken and only God could put it together again. I was stepping out in faith, God was in control, I was being lead by the Holy Spirit and I had to take the first step. I walked into his office expecting the usual reaction and I was not disappointed. When I spoke it was as if the wind was blowing, when I was in the room it was as if I were invisible, totally discounted.

"I wrote a book about Heidi and our family. Do you want to read it?"

Larry looked at me with a vacant stare. I laid it on his desk and walked out. I was praying the entire time. "God, it is all in Your hands, I give this entire situation to You, may Your will be done."

Later in the afternoon, I walked by Larry's office and he was sitting reading the book. When I left that evening for home, I walked by his office again, and he was still reading the book. When I came into the office the next day, the manuscript was lying on my desk. Was this a crack in the wall?

What day it was, what time it was and how things came around I could not tell you, but there was a change. God was working and I did not understand how, when, or where, I only knew it was huge to me, to our family. It was a parting of the Red Sea. Larry started building a gate in his wall. He was still protecting his property but the gate was definitely going in. There was a change, a definite distinctive change, obvious to all. I continued to pray and thank God for His amazing mercy on our family.

Since that day in March, our family is talking and spending some time together. Michelle and her children are back in church as she is settling into being a single mom. Larry is spending time and sharing with his father and me again. Larry and Haydon have started coming over again and grandpa gets to pick Haydon up more often. Larry has not decided to return to church, yet he continues to trust God for healing.

Larry Sr. is very angry with God and has stopped attending church and Life Group all together. He still struggles to understand God's ways. I continue to hope and pray and trust God to complete a good work in him. Each one of us continues on our own journey yet we are working hard at sharing our feelings and thoughts and not judging each other.

If this book accomplished nothing but the beginning of reconciliation for my family, then the hand of God has touched us with His mercy and His purpose is being accomplished in our lives. My prayer for anyone who has read this book, would be to accept Jesus Christ as their Lord and Savior and know wherever they are in this journey called life that God loves them and if you will choose to turn everything over to God, He will take all the hurt and heartache and work it out for something good and wonderful in your life.

In His time, in His way, for your eternal good, just trust Him. It is not easy, that is why life is called a journey and not a destination. A journey is a passage from one place to another, always moving, always changing; it is a process. If this life were the destination, then there would be no purpose for a journey. I am excited about this journey with all of its valleys and mountaintops for I continue on with the assurance my destination is *home*.

May your life's journey from this day forward be guided by the Word of God, filled with the Holy Spirit, and lived with the gift of salvation through Jesus. Continue on your journey with the knowledge Jesus will be waiting for you at *home*.

Our Journey's Continue . . .

Marsha R. Nix
Anaheim, California
2005

Author Biography

Author Marsha Nix and her husband of 40 years, Larry Sr., have two children, Larry and Michelle. They are also the grandparents of six amazing children (three boys, two girls, and one girl in Heaven). Marsha has been a business owner for 35 years. She has seen life on top of the mountain with the light shining brightly and has experienced life at its ugliest, in the deepest darkest hole. She currently resides in Anaheim, California, and has been president of their family business for the past 14 years. Marsha enjoys traveling, reading, gardening, and running. Running has become a way to reach a goal when all else is falling down around.

Contact Marsha Nix
marshan@heidihugs.com

or order more copies of this book at

TATE PUBLISHING, LLC

127 East Trade Center Terrace
Mustang, OK 73064

888.361.9473

Tate Publishing, LLC

www.tatepublishing.com